My Brilliant Friend: A Guide for Book Clubs

KATHRYN COPE

ISBN: 1534727140
ISBN-13: 978-1534727144

CONTENTS

INTRODUCTION

There are few things more rewarding than getting together with a group of like-minded people and discussing a good book. Book club meetings, at their best, are vibrant, passionate affairs. Each member will bring along a different perspective and ideally there will be heated debate.

A surprising number of book club members, however, report that their meetings have been a disappointment. Even though their group loved the particular book they were discussing, they could think of astonishingly little to say about it. Failing to find interesting discussion angles for a book is the single most common reason for book group discussions to fall flat. Most book groups only meet once a month and a lacklustre meeting is frustrating for everyone.

The Reading Room Book Group Guides were born out of a passion for book clubs. Packed with information, they take the hard work out of preparing for a meeting and ensure that your book group discussions never run dry. How you choose to use the guides is entirely up to you. The author biography, literary style and historical context sections provide useful background information which may be interesting to share with your group at the beginning of your meeting. The all-important list of discussion questions, which will probably form the core of your meeting, can be found towards the end of this guide. To support your responses to the discussion questions, you may find it helpful to refer to the 'Themes & Imagery' and 'Character' sections.

A detailed plot synopsis is provided as an *aide-memoire* if you need to recap on the finer points of the plot. There is also a quick quiz - a fun way to test your knowledge and bring your discussion to a close. Finally, if this was a book that you particularly enjoyed, the guide concludes with a list of books similar in style or subject matter.

1

Be warned, this guide contains spoilers. Please do not be tempted to read it before you have read the original novel as plot surprises will be well and truly ruined.

Kathryn Cope, 2016

ELENA FERRANTE

Elena Ferrante is the pen name of an Italian novelist whose true identity is not publicly known. She has kept her identity secret since the publication of her first novel in 1992. As *Troubling Love* was about to be published the author made it clear to her publisher that she would not take part in any publicity other than an occasional written interview. Even the American Italian translator of Ferrante's novels, Ann Goldstein, claims not to know Ferrante's true identity and has stood in for the Italian author at publicity events.

Ferrante's authorial anonymity is a bold statement in a literary world which increasingly revolves around marketing and publicity. In written interviews she has explained that her decision to remain anonymous is motivated by the belief that books, 'once they are written, have no need of their authors' as they take on 'an intense life of their own.' She has also pointed out that anonymity gives her 'a space of absolute creative freedom' in which she can explore subject matter which is personally painful to her or, as she puts it, stick 'a finger in certain wounds I have that are still infected'.

Ironically, while Ferrante hoped that her anonymity would focus attention away from her and towards her books, it seems to have had the reverse effect. The mystery surrounding her identity has led to many rumours in literary circles. Could her novels be the product of a collaboration of authors? Or, most contentiously, could the Italian novels that speak so eloquently of female experience have been written by a man? This last rumour has led to a theory in Italy that Ferrante's novels might be the work of the male avant-garde novelist Domenico Starnone.

While her official website reveals only that she was born in Naples, Ferrante has revealed a little more about herself in correspondence with journalists. The theory that Ferrante is a man is contradicted by her reference to herself as a mother. She has also revealed that she does not come from a wealthy background and found 'climbing the economic ladder' a struggle. Other than this,

3

she has revealed that she has a classics degree and, as well as writing, translates and teaches for a living. Ferrante's reluctance to reveal any more about herself has led critics to assume that her work is largely autobiographical. Much has been made of her decision to give the narrator of her Neapolitan novels the name Elena and several of her novels address the conflicting demands of being a writer and a mother.

Whatever the truth about Ferrante's identity, there is no doubt that her novels have struck a powerful chord with many readers. Fellow novelists Zadie Smith, Jhumpa Lahiri and Claire Messud have all extravagantly praised her work while the hashtag #FerranteFever reflects the Italian author's devoted following, particularly among an English-language readership.

All of Ferrante's novels are narrated by women and chronicle female experience in a sometimes shockingly frank way. While she portrays women at different stages of experience (pubescent girls, abused or abandoned wives, mothers, grandmothers, widows), their lives are always difficult and conflicted. Caught within the confines of the traditional domestic roles assigned to women, her characters often begin to unravel. While there is, perhaps, nothing new about Ferrante's subject matter it is the way she addresses it that gives her work its unique quality. Nothing is prettified for the sake of art: sex, jealousy, motherhood, and child abuse are all described with a fierce honesty and the rage of the women who experience them make the narratives crackle with a raw energy.

Troubling Love
(Italian publication 1992, English translation 2006)

This disturbing novel is an exploration of mother/daughter relationships. After her mother drowns, Delia, the narrator, receives a number of mysterious phone calls which cast a different light on the days leading up to her mother's death. Focusing mainly on the day of the funeral in Naples, Ferrante describes Delia's fraught state-of-mind as she roams the city thinking about her childhood and her ambivalent feelings towards her mother. The novel was adapted into the film 'Nasty Love' directed by Mario Martone.

4

The Days of Abandonment
(Italian publication 2002, English translation 2005)

Ferrante's first novel is an intense insight into the mind of a woman who finds herself abandoned by her husband. Holed up in her apartment in the middle of a heatwave, Olga, the middle-aged narrator, descends into near-madness after her husband leaves her for a much younger woman. The novel was adapted into a film of the same title directed by Roberto Faenza.

The Lost Daughter
(Italian publication 2006, English translation 2008)

Leda, an English professor, is divorced from her husband and her daughters have gone to live with their father in Canada. While alone on holiday she begins to observe a beautiful young woman, Nina, with her husband and her daughter, Elena. Leda's interest becomes an obsession and, as she watches the family, she is reminded of incidents in her life where her own lack of maternal instincts became apparent. Events come to a head when Leda finds Elena's lost doll and decides, for her own reasons, not to return it.

The Neapolitan Quartet

Ferrante has become best known for her series of Neapolitan novels. Translated into English, these are *My Brilliant Friend* (2012), *The Story of a New Name* (2013), *Those Who Leave and Those Who Stay* (2014), and *The Story of the Lost Child* (2015). The four novels follow the lives of two friends, Elena and Lila, from their childhood in a poverty-stricken area of Naples in the 1950s to their old age. Like her previous novels, the Neapolitan quartet paints an intense portrait of women's domestic lives. Elena and Lila are two extremely intelligent girls and the story describes their attempts to forge a meaningful identity in a world where they are restricted by both gender roles and class. In these novels, however, the characters' struggles are also set within the wider context of Italian history. The conflicts in the women's lives reflect the political and economic changes that took place in Italy in the late twentieth century.

While Ferrante's earlier novels were appreciated by the literary

5

few in the know, the Neapolitan series went from a favourite of critics to bestseller in the course of twelve months. Gripped by the characters of Elena and Lila and their enduring yet disturbing friendship, readers couldn't wait to get their hands on the next instalment. So addictive is the series that Ferrante fans admitted to both looking forward to and dreading the publication of the final book in the quartet. *My Brilliant Friend* was shortlisted for the Waterstones Book of the Year 2015 and the fourth book of the quartet, *The Story of the Lost Child*, appeared on the New York Times 10 Best Books of 2015.

PLOT SUMMARY

PROLOGUE

Eliminating All the Traces

Chapter 1

Elena Greco receives a phone call from Rino, the son of her friend, Lila. Rino declares that his sixty-six-year-old mother has been missing for two weeks and asks if she is with Elena in Turin. Elena is incredulous at the stupidity of this question as Lila has never ventured beyond the area of Naples. Rino says that his mother has been behaving even more erratically than usual lately and begins to cry. Elena tells him not to look for his mother and to stand on his own two feet. She hangs up.

Chapter 2

Elena reveals that Lila's real name is Rafaella Cerullo and others call her Lina, but, to her only, she has always been Lila. Elena is unsurprised at her friend's disappearance as Lila told her three decades earlier that she wanted 'to disappear without leaving a trace'.

Chapter 3

Elena reveals that she has deliberately thrown away any mementoes of her friend. She calls Rino who confirms that his mother has removed every one of her possessions from the house and has even cut herself out of all the photographs. Rino asks if he can come and stay with Elena but she flatly refuses. Angry at her friend, she reflects that Lila 'is overdoing it as usual'. She begins to

7

write the story of their childhood announcing, 'We'll see who wins this time'.

CHILDHOOD

The Story of Don Achille

Chapter 1

Elena recalls the birth of her friendship with Lila. It happens when the girls are eight years old and they courageously decide to visit Don Achille's apartment. Don Achille is feared and hated by the adults of the neighborhood for reasons not fully understood by the children and Elena imagines him as a hideous ogre. Terrified, Elena believes that Don Achille will kill them but she follows Lila, hoping that her friend will change her mind. On the way, Lila stops and gives Elena her hand: a gesture which cements their relationship.

Chapter 2

Elena remembers that, a few weeks earlier, she and Lila were playing separately in a courtyard with their dolls. Finally acknowledging each other, they exchange dolls and Lila deliberately drops Elena's doll, Tina, down a grate into the cellar below.

Chapter 3

Elena first gets to know Lila at school in first grade. Lila impresses Elena by being openly badly behaved in full view of their teacher, Maestra Oliviero. During one particularly memorable incident, Lila refuses to obey the teacher's order to stand behind the blackboard. As she storms towards Lila, Maestra Oliviero trips and hits her face on the corner of a desk. Elena is shocked to see her teacher lying on the floor as if she is dead.

One day after school, a group of boys, led by Enzo, throw rocks at Lila and Elena. Elena runs away but Lila stands her ground. Although, at this point, the girls haven't yet spoken to each other, Elena goes back to Lila and hands her some stones to throw at the boys. Lila hits Enzo with a sharp rock, making his leg gush with blood. Elena tries to pull Lila away but Enzo throws a rock

8

which cuts Lila's head and knocks her to the sidewalk.

Chapter 4

Elena's father often rants about his hatred of Don Achille but it is well known in the neighborhood that Achille's true enemy is Signor Peluso, the carpenter. Peluso blames his financial ruin on Don Achille, accusing him of taking his carpenter's shop and turning it into a grocery store. When Elena is in second grade, a rumour spreads that Signor Peluso screamed at Don Achille outside the local Catholic Church. In response, Don Achille picked Signor Peluso up and threw him against a tree, leaving him barely conscious.

Chapter 5

Melina Cappuccio, a distant relative of Lila's mother, lives in the same building as Elena's family and is prone to episodes of mental illness. Although only thirty years old, Melina is widowed and has six children. After the death of Melina's husband, Donato Sarratore, a married man who lived in the apartment above, offered her help and support. Melina's gratitude turned into love, however, and she began to persecute Donato's wife, Lidia. One day Elena witnesses Melina and Lidia fighting. The women roll down the stairs and Melina's head hits the floor of the landing right by her foot. On another occasion, Elena, Lila and Marisa Sarratore see Melina in the street and Marisa insults her. Lila, who always shows empathy for the unfortunate widow, slaps Marisa hard and goes to speak to Melina. Elena is shocked when she realises that Melina is eating soap out of a paper bag.

Chapter 6

Following Maestra Oliviero's classroom accident, both the teacher and Lila disappear from the class for some time. When the teacher returns to school Elena notices that she begins to praise Lila. On one occasion Lila's mother, Nunzia, calls into school with a gift of sugar and coffee for Maestra Oliviero. The teacher accepts the gifts and tells Nunzia that, although her six-year-old daughter is the worst behaved child in the class, she has recently discovered that

9

she is also the cleverest. Maestra Oliviero gets Lila to demonstrate that she can already read and write. Nunzia, who is semi-literate at best, tells the teacher that no one has been helping Lila at home and Lila confirms that she has taught himself to read.

Chapter 7

While Elena feels loved by her father and younger siblings, she feels neglected by her mother. In return, Elena feels repulsion for her mother's limp and wayward right eye. To compensate, Elena revels in the attention of Maestra Oliviero who encourages and makes a fuss of her at school. When Maestra Oliviero begins to favour Lila in the classroom, Elena feels as if she has been demoted. Noticing that Lila's legs are 'always moving', she begins to become preoccupied with the idea that her own legs will stop working properly. Elena resolves to keep pace with Lila's achievements in the belief that it will ward off inheriting her mother's limp.

Chapter 8

Elena devotes herself to studying in an attempt to keep up with Lila, although she soon realises that even with her best efforts, she will always come second to her. The two girls are a complete contrast to each other in appearance and manner. While Elena is fair, pretty and eager to please, Lila is dark, unhealthily skinny and aggressive. When they are in second grade, Maestro Oliviero often takes the girls into Maestro Ferraro's class to compete with the fourth grade students in a mental maths competition. On these occasions Elena is surprised to notice that Nino Sarratore (the boy she believes she loves) answers very few questions. Even more surprisingly, Alfonso (the youngest son of Don Achille) and Enzo (who has a reputation for being lazy and stupid) both demonstrate a considerable skill for mental arithmetic. Elena realises that Lila is reluctant to publicly compete with the son of Don Achille and often holds back in his presence. One day, however, Lila is spurred on by Enzo's contributions and competes in earnest. After beating Alfonso, Lila continues a mathematical duel with Enzo and eventually wins the competition. Enzo is furious and shouts obscenities at Lila. It is from this point that the boys begin to

10

throw rocks at Lila.

Chapter 9

After the maths competition, Alfonso goes home in tears. The next day Alfonso's older brother, Stefano, comes to school and pushes Lila against a wall, threatening to grab her tongue and prick it with a pin. Stefano also assaults Enzo. In retaliation Lila's brother, Rino, starts a fight with Stefano. A few days later Don Achille's wife, Maria, insults Lila's mother. To bring hostilities to a close Lila's father publicly apologises to Don Achille.

The stone-throwing incident between Enzo and Lila ends with Enzo crying when he sees the cut on Lila's head. Rino later beats Enzo up outside school.

Chapter 10

Lila begins to subject Elena to 'proofs of courage', culminating in the day when she drops Elena's doll into the cellar. Although Elena is distressed by the loss of her doll she is careful not to show it and throws Lila's doll down too. The two girls go down to the cellar together to search for the dolls but fail to find them. They conclude that Don Achille must have taken them and put them in his black bag.

Chapter 11

After the cellar incident Elena is haunted by the image of Don Achille as a grotesque monster carrying the head of her doll. Exhausted by anxiety and the strain of trying to keep up with Lila, she becomes ill and goes through a period of 'tactile dysfunction' where solid surfaces feel soft or distorted.

Shortly afterwards, Nino pushes Elena against a wall and tells her that he wants her to become engaged to him. Although Elena is in love with Nino, her anxiety causes her to rebuff him and run away. After this she avoids him.

One day the Sarratore family begin to move all of their belongings out of their apartment. Elena's mother speculates that they are moving to escape Melina's persecution of Lidia Sarratore and, as they watch, Melina begins screaming and throwing

11

household items out of her window at the Sarratore family. Nino narrowly escapes being killed as the final missile (a steel iron) lands a few inches away from him.

Chapter 12

While Elena has become popular with boys, she observes that nobody has ever declared their love to Lila. After the rock throwing incident, however, Enzo presents Lila with a token of his respect: a garland of sorb apples.

Chapter 13

Near the end of the fifth grade, Maestra Oliviera tells Elena, Lila and their classmate Gigliola that they have the aptitude to continue their schooling. The teacher calls the girls' parents in and urges them to let their daughters take the admissions test for middle school. Elena's mother is initially opposed to the idea and begrudges the money they will have to pay for extra tuition. Her parents finally agree on the proviso that they will take Elena out of school to work if she doesn't do well. Lila's father refuses to even discuss the idea of his daughter continuing with her studies, although Rino argues that he is making a mistake. Undeterred, Maestra Oliviero insists that Lila's mother comes into school to see examples of her daughter's brilliant work. Nunzia does as she is asked but continues to refuse consent as she cannot overrule her husband. Nevertheless, Lila tells Elena that she intends to take the admissions test anyway.

Chapter 14

Lila and Elena climb the stairs to Don Achille's apartment to ask for their dolls back. When Don Achille comes to the door, he turns out to be 'ugly' but not in the monstrous way Elena imagined. Lila accuses Don Achille of taking their dolls from the cellar. Bemused, he hands them some money and tells them to buy new dolls.

Chapter 15

Elena and Gigliola start private lessons with Maestra Oliviera to

12

prepare for the admissions test. Rino is still trying to persuade his father to let Lina take the admissions test, suggesting that if they pay him for the work he does in the shoe repair shop, he will pay for his sister to go to school. Lila adores her brother and is confident that he will eventually win the battle on her behalf.

Lila buys a copy of *Little Women* with the money from Don Achille and she regularly meets with Elena in the courtyard so they can read it together. Lila and Elena become obsessed with wealth and often talk about what they will do when they are rich. They begin to believe that, if they study hard, they will be able to write books similar to *Little Women* and make lots of money. When Lila suggests that they write a book together, Elena agrees but wants to start the project after she has taken the admissions test. Lila cannot wait, however, and begins to write a story called 'The Blue Fairy' while Elena is having private lessons. When Lila presents her friend with the story, Elena is hurt but also struck by the brilliance of Lila's writing. At her next private lesson, Elena gives the story to Maestra Oliviero to read but the teacher responds with cold disinterest. A few days later, Elena asks her teacher if she has read Lila's story. Maestra Oliviero doesn't answer but implies that Lila's family are 'plebs'. She advises Elena to forget about Lila and concentrate on her own education. Lila assumes from the teacher's silence that her story had no merit. She becomes subdued as, even in class, Maestra Oliviero has stopped praising her.

Chapter 16

One day, just before the admissions tests, Lila encourages Elena to skip school so that they can follow a road which Rino has told her leads to the sea. Elena follows Lila's instructions, telling her mother that she will be late home as she is going to a party at her teacher's house after school.

Although the girls have never walked beyond the neighborhood before, Elena is confident in Lila's leadership. As they become tired and thirsty, however, Elena notices that her friend looks increasingly uncertain. When it begins to rain Lila insists that they turn back, although Elena wants to continue to the sea. They run home and Elena is confronted by her mother who has been searching for her for hours after discovering her daughter had lied about the party. Elena's mother insists that her father should give

13

her a beating as punishment. Elena's father is reluctant to do so and, in the ensuing argument, ends up hitting his wife and his daughter.

The next day Elena is frustrated at being punished without even having achieved her goal and struggles to understand why she and Lila never reached the sea. She realises that the incident marks a reversal in her relationship with Lila. While she had been the courageous one, eager to continue with their adventure, Lila had been frightened by her unfamiliar surroundings. When Elena sees Lila her friend seems surprised to learn that Elena's parents are still allowing her to continue with her private lessons. Elena wonders whether Lila planned the episode in the hope that it would ruin her chances of going to middle school.

Chapter 17

Towards the end of the academic year Elena notices that Lila seems to have lost her drive. While Elena gets tens in the final tests at elementary school, Lila's scores are less impressive.

Elena becomes jealous when Lila begins to spend most of her time with Carmela Peluso. The girls become 'a trio' in which Elena always feels 'the third'. Although neither she nor Carmela have taken the admission test for middle school, Lila still stubbornly refers to the time when they will all go to middle school together. One day Elena points out that it is impossible for Lila and Carmela to join her at middle school as they haven't taken the admissions test. Lila insists that they will go all the same and begins to pester her family to pay for her to study Latin like Elena. One day Elena goes to call for her friend and, from outside, hears ten-year-old Lila aggressively insulting her father. A moment later, Signor Cerullo throws his daughter out of the apartment window. Lila tries to get up, claiming to be unhurt, but she is bleeding and has a broken arm.

Chapter 18

The violent atmosphere of the neighborhood comes to a head when Don Achille is found murdered in his own home. Lila is obsessed with the incident and tells the story every day as if she were there when it happened, describing everything from the stab

14

wound in his neck to his spurting blood hitting a copper pot that hung on the wall. She is also convinced that the murderer was a woman.

One day Elena and Lila are at Carmela's house playing cards when the carabinieri arrive and arrest Alfredo Peluso. As they take him away, Alfredo struggles and swears he is innocent.

ADOLESCENCE

The Story of the Shoes

Chapter 1

Elena describes Lila's first episode of 'dissolving margins'. Although the incident took place in 1958 on New Year's Eve, Lila only told Elena about it in 1980 when they were both married thirty-six-year-old women with children of their own. Lila's strange experience took place on the roof terrace of an apartment building as she watched the neighborhood boys setting off fireworks. On hearing gunshots and Rino shouting obscenities, she was suddenly overcome with a horrifying sense that the human outlines of those around her were dissolving.

Chapter 2

After Lila's broken arm heals, her father decides that she should be allowed to study stenography, bookkeeping and home economics. Lila is unenthusiastic and her parents are often called in by her new teachers as she is disruptive and often absent. She appears to 'willingly' succumb to a bout of flu and Elena becomes anxious at rumours that her friend might die. Eventually Lila recovers but fails her school assessments at the end of the year.

When Elena starts middle school she is initially pleased that Lila isn't there to outshine her. She quickly discovers, however, that many of the other students are better than her. Alfonso Carracci, for example, also attends the school and Elena hears rumours that he is extremely clever. Struggling not to end up at the bottom of the class, Elena begins to feel that her inferior performance is due to Lila's absence.

At the end of the academic year Gigliola has to repeat Latin and

15

mathematics while Elena passes with mediocre scores. One of the teachers calls Elena's mother into school and tells her that her daughter will not pass Latin the following year without private lessons. Elena's mother argues that, as the teachers aren't happy with Elena, she should leave school and help her in the house. After an argument, however, Elena's father decides that, as she has passed everything, she deserves to continue in school.

Elena is despondent during the summer holidays believing that Lila no longer wants to be her friend. One day she discovers that her underpants are stained with blood. Too frightened and ashamed to tell her mother, Elena bumps into Lila and Carmela and blurts out what has happened to her. Carmela, who has already been menstruating for a year, reassures Elena that the bleeding is normal and means that she is now a grown-up. When asked, Lila reluctantly admits that she hasn't menstruated yet and Elena suddenly notices how small and physically underdeveloped Lila is. From this point Elena becomes very friendly with Carmela, while Lila seems to avoid them. Carmela confides that she is in love with Alfonso Carracci. Elena is deeply struck by the romantic notion of the daughter of a murderer falling in love with the son of the victim.

Chapter 3

As her body changes into that of a young woman, Elena becomes anxious and unhappy. One day Gino, the pharmacist's son, approaches her claiming that he has bet twenty lire that her breasts are real. He says that if she proves him correct, he will give ten lire to her. Elena is frightened and tries to behave in the way she imagines Lila would in this situation. She asks for the ten lire and then displays her breasts to Gino and one of his classmates.

Chapter 4

Rino makes Lila return to her school but, again, she rarely attends and fails. Elena scarcely sees her friend who begins to spend her time helping her parents in the house and in the shoe repair shop. On the rare occasions when she sees her, Lila talks only about shoe repairs: a world which she seems completely immersed in. Elena begins to feel that she is wasting her time at school and envies Lila

16

when she sees her working in the shoe shop.

Chapter 5

One day Elena secretly follows Lila into their old elementary school and discovers that her friend is borrowing books from a lending library run by Maestro Ferraro. Lila has never mentioned this to Elena and never talks to her about what she has read.

Elena's mother declares that her daughter's big breasts are 'indecent' and takes her to buy a bra. Suddenly very popular with the opposite sex, she discovers that Gino and his friends have told the other boys about their encounter and several more boys approach her, asking to see her breasts. Elena begins to cross her arms to conceal her chest and feels guilty. She rarely leaves the house and studies hard.

Gino asks Elena to be his girlfriend on several occasions but she refuses. When Lila asks why she has turned Gino down, Elena claims she is not sure of her feelings: a phrase she has learned from the photo magazines she reads with Carmela. Lila convinces Elena that she can only be sure of Gino's love by subjecting him to a series of tests. She advises Elena to become Gino's girlfriend on the condition that he buys ice cream for them all summer. Elena does as she advises and Gino immediately loses interest. Carmela tells the other neighborhood girls about Lila's wise relationship advice to Elena and Lila becomes a kind of agony aunt for girls who want advice about love. Elena is surprised to observe that she seems to embrace the role.

Chapter 6

At the end of the academic year Elena is humiliated to discover that she has failed Latin and both Alfonso and Gigliola have higher scores than her. When Elena's father learns that she must retake Latin in September, he decides it is pointless for her to continue with school as they do not have the money for private lessons. Elena is devastated. Later, however, Elena's mother tells her that she can continue with her education if she passes Latin without private lessons. When Lila discovers that Elena is retaking Latin, she asks a favour of her: to meet her once a day in the public gardens with her Latin books.

17

Chapter 7

Elena notices that the face of the neighborhood has changed in recent years as small businesses have begun to flourish. Enzo has taken over his parents' fruit and vegetable business, Bar Solara has become a pastry shop, and the grocery, run by Don Achille's widow, has expanded into a delicatessen. The rising prosperity of the Solara family is flaunted by the Solara brothers, Marcello and Michele, who drive around the neighborhood in a Fiat 1100.

As Elena studies with Lila, it becomes clear that her friend already knows a great deal of Latin. Lila reluctantly admits that she has taken out a library card in the name of each member of her family and, during Elena's first year in middle school, she studied Latin grammar from a library book. Lila assigns Elena homework and suggests her friend tries a different translation technique. As a result, Elena easily passes her exam in September. Grateful to her friend, Elena suggest that they continue studying together but Lila says that, as she now understands Latin, she feels no further need to study it. Claiming that she has important business to conduct with Rino, Lila says that Elena will now have to study on her behalf.

Chapter 8

Now thirteen years old, Elena returns to school. Motivated at the thought of studying on Lila's behalf, she excels in all her subjects, becoming top of the class.

One day Elena is approached by the Solara brothers in their car who tell her to get in for a ride. Elena declines and the Solara brothers politely accept her answer. Shortly afterwards it becomes common knowledge that the Solara brothers pulled Melina's fourteen-year-old daughter, Ada, into their car and brought her back an hour later. When Ada's older brother, Antonio, learns of the incident he lies in wait for the brothers and attacks them. Antonio is badly beaten by the brothers and their father but no one dares intervene. Many of the girls in the neighborhood, including Gigliola and Carmela, admire the handsome Solara brothers and take their side. Although Elena also finds the brothers attractive, she feels that they behaved badly towards Ada. Lila is furious when she hears of the incident.

Lila tells Elena that she and Rino are trying to persuade their father to expand his business to include making handmade shoes. She shows Elena the beautiful shoe designs she has drawn and explains that she plans to make a single pair of the shoes to convince her father. Once that is done, she eventually plans to set up a Cerullo shoe factory in order to raise her family out of poverty. Lila goes on to point out that the Solara brothers treated Ada without respect because she comes from a poor family. She argues that she and Elena either have to make more money than the Solara family or do them serious harm in some other way. Lila is confident that the brothers won't attempt to touch her because she is 'ugly' but insists that if they try to touch Elena, she must tell her immediately.

Chapter 9

At the end of middle school Elena passes her exam with flying colours. Her parents are proud of her and, as a reward, her mother says she can wear her silver bracelet on Sunday. Elena's pride in her achievements is spoiled, however, when Lila only expresses disappointment that she didn't get tens.

Elena is going through a physically awkward stage and feels unattractive. She becomes reclusive, helping her mother around the house and spending her free time reading books borrowed from the library. One day she receives an invitation from Maestro Ferraro to an awards ceremony at the library to honour its most prolific readers. Lila doesn't attend the ceremony and when Elena is awarded fifth prize (a copy of *Three Men in a Boat* by Jerome K Jerome), she also collects the other winners' awards on behalf of Lila and all her family. Elena bumps into Maestra Oliviero at the ceremony who praises Elena's academic achievements and asks what she is going to do next. Elena explains that her parents expect her to go to work but Maestra Oliviero insists that she must continue studying and announces that she will talk to Elena's parents about it. She also observes that Elena was giggling with Pasquale Peluso throughout the ceremony. Maestra Oliviero advises Elena not to waste her time with Pasquale as he is a construction worker and will never amount to anything. After the ceremony Pasquale asks Elena if she and Lila would like to join him and his sister at Gigliola's house to learn to dance. He also

19

suggests that they meet up the next day so that they can deliver the library prizes to Rino and Lila. Despite her teacher's advice, Elena agrees, flattered by Pasquale's apparent interest in her.

Chapter 10

True to her word, Maestra Oliviero visits Elena's parents and makes them promise that they will enroll her in the nearest classical high school. In return, she will provide any books that Elena needs. Elena's parents are furious but too intimidated by Maestra Oliviero to say no.

Elena and her family hear a commotion from Melina's apartment. On questioning the neighbours they discover that the widow is jumping on her bed and pulling up her skirt, showing her underpants to her frightened children. Elena's mother goes to investigate and reports that Melina's joyful delirium has been prompted by the delivery of a book of poems by Donato Sarratore. Sarratore has sent the book to Melina with a written inscription to her inside. Elena is greatly affected by the news. The knowledge that someone from the neighborhood has published a book makes her believe that it may be possible for her to live out her dream and do the same.

Chapter 11

On the way to the shoe shop Pasquale asks Elena questions about Lila and, when they arrive, Elena notices Pasquale looking 'furtively' at her friend. Elena excitedly tells Lila about Melina and the poetry book. Lila produces the book and explains that Melina's eldest son, Antonio, has given it to her to keep it out of reach of his mother. She points out to Elena that the poetry book has done more harm than good, as Melina will now expect a visit from Donato and will be devastated if he doesn't appear. Elena comes to the unpleasant realisation that Pasquale arranged to meet her only so he could see Lila.

Chapter 12

Lila tells Elena that she and Rino are working together on a man's travelling shoe, keeping it secret from their father. Elena feels

20

dejected as her friend is immersed in a world that she cannot be a part of. When she tells Lila that she is going to high school, Lila questions her about it before muttering that she has finally got her period.

Chapter 13

Elena is disquieted at the thought that Lila is changing into a young woman and reflects that Pasquale must have noticed before she did. In the light of Lila's news, Elena's educational triumphs suddenly seem less impressive.

One Sunday afternoon Elena wears her best dress and her mother's silver bracelet when she goes to meet Lila. As the two girls are walking along, the Solara brothers pull up in their car and try to persuade them to get in. During the exchange Marcello grabs Elena's arm through the window and points out to his brother that 'the porter's daughter' is wearing a nice bracelet. The bracelet breaks and Elena panics about what her mother's reaction will be. Marcello gets out of the car, saying that he will fix it for her, and touches Elena's wrist in a calming gesture. In response, Lila holds a sharp shoemaker's knife to Marcello's throat and warns him not to touch her friend. Michele initially laughs at Lila but, when the knife begins to draw blood, realises that she is serious. He tells his brother to apologise to the ladies and get in the car. Marcello quickly repairs the bracelet and apologises to Lila.

Chapter 14

Elena feels that her world is expanding when her father takes her into the city and shows her the sights. When she glimpses Vesuvius and the sea at close quarters, the spectacular sight seems to represent all the promise that life holds for her and Lila. Elena tells Lila about the experience later but her friend doesn't seem interested in hearing about the world beyond their neighborhood.

Lila develops an interest in dancing and starts taking Elena to the little parties at Gigliola's house. One day the girls are practising their steps together when Lila points out that the word gramophone is Greek. Elena is confused until she spots Lila's Greek grammar book on the side. She makes an excuse and abruptly leaves.

21

Chapter 15

Elena is angry that Lila has begun to study Greek before she has even started high school. She goes to the library to borrow a Greek grammar only to find that the entire Cerullo family are borrowing it in succession. Feeling 'diminished' by her friend once again, Elena briefly considers erasing Lila from her life before giving in to the urge to see her. Lila insists that Elena should start learning the Greek alphabet before she begins school.

While Elena is covered in pimples and feels unattractive, Lila is blossoming into a graceful and beautiful young woman. When they go dancing Elena notices that the local boys cannot keep their eyes off Lila.

Chapter 16

Elena notices that Lila's presence often acts as the catalyst for violence among the opposite sex. One night, when they go out to a pizzeria, Rino slaps the pizza maker across the face for blowing a kiss to his sister. On another occasion, they go to a cafe and a man who has been sitting with his family comes over to the table and compliments Lila on her beauty. Rino is furious and marches the man back to his table where he aggressively insults him in front of his wife and family.

Elena recalls one of the worst episodes, which takes place at a party, when she and Lila are fourteen years old. During the party tensions rise as Enzo, Stefano, Pasquale and Marcello Solara all compete to dance with Lila. When Pasquale dances with Lila, Michele accuses Stefano of being 'a sissy' for letting the son of the man who killed his father humiliate him. Elena is then astonished when Lila agrees to dance with Marcello, as she knows her friend detests him. While they are dancing, Pasquale storms over to Elena and says they have to go, deliberately bumping into Michele on the way out. When Lila starts to follow Elena, Marcello grasps her arm and urges her to stay for another dance. In response, Lila looks at Marcello as if she has only just realised who he is and tries to free herself. Striding in to help Lila, Enzo grabs Marcello's wrist and he forces him to let go. Once they are outside, Pasquale begins a furious rant about the Solara brothers and Stefano. Pasquale claims that the Bar Solara is a favoured hangout for villains including loan

22

sharks from the Camorra, smugglers and corrupt politicians. He also says that Don Achille was a spy for the Nazi Fascists and the money Stefano was using to expand the grocery store was made by his father on the black market. Declaring that his father was right to kill Don Achille, Pasquale threatens to kill the rest of his family and cut the throats of the Solara brothers. Spurred on by Pasquale's speech, Antonio expresses his rage at the way the Solara brothers disrespected his sister, Ada. Despite Enzo's attempts to calm them down, Pasquale and Antonio become determined to confront the Solara brothers when they leave the party. It is only when Pasquale sees Lila crying that he changes his mind and says he will settle them another time. On the way home Lila interrogates Pasquale about the meanings of Nazi Fascism and the black market.

Chapter 17

Lila is strongly affected by what she learns from Pasquale and becomes obsessed with the idea that everything in the neighborhood is founded on a historical chain of corruption. As she starts reading up on the subject, her political knowledge soon surpasses that of Pasquale and he hangs on Lila's every word. Elena confidently expects them to fall in love and get married.

Chapter 18

Elena starts high school, along with Alfonso and Gino. She finds the work difficult and follows a rigidly disciplined study programme, largely in an attempt to impress Lila. Elena's teacher, Professor Gerace, is impressed by Lila's proficiency in Greek, thanks to the studying she did with Lila over the holidays. Word spreads among the teachers that Elena is a gifted student.

Elena is determined to find a boyfriend before Lila makes the inevitable announcement that she is going with Pasquale, or one of the other young men who admire her. One day she spots an older boy at school and realises it is Nino Sarratore. Nino appears not to recognise Elena and she becomes obsessed with catching a glimpse of him at school. One day Gino asks Elena to be his girlfriend. Although Elena believes him to be an idiot, she agrees out of desperation.

Lila is preoccupied with Melina's evident decline into

23

depression and madness. She instructs Elena to talk to Nino and make him tell his father about Melina's state of mind.

Chapter 19

Now that Elena is doing well at high school and has a boyfriend, she begins to feel superior to Lila. The feeling lasts only until Lila shows Elena her new project: a beautiful pair of men's shoes that she and her brother have made together.

Chapter 20

In 1958, as New Year approaches, Lila becomes increasingly concerned about her brother's state of mind. Believing that the shoe-making business will make him rich, Rino becomes obsessed with wanting to make more money than the Solara brothers, who he envies and dislikes. This preoccupation is demonstrated in his determination to set off more fireworks than the Solara brothers on New Year's Eve.

One day, when Elena goes to the grocery shop with Lina, they receive an unexpected invitation from Stefano to celebrate New Year at his house. Elena tells him they are planning to celebrate with Rino and his friends but Stefano insists that they also invite Lila's brother. When Lila points out that Pasquale, Carmen and their mother were also invited, Stefano surprisingly extends the invitation to the family of the man who allegedly murdered his father. He promises an impressive fireworks display.

Chapter 21

Elena teases Lila saying that Stefano is holding the party just for her. Lila disagrees, believing that Stefano's extended invitation to the neighborhood is a gesture of forgiveness and an indication that he wants to draw a line under past family feuds. Persuaded by this argument, all the local families agree to go.

Chapter 22

On New Year's Eve there is a battle between the fireworks at Stefano's party and those being lit nearby by the Solara brothers.

24

The contest becomes increasingly frenzied as the young men, led by Rino, light more and more fireworks and shout insults at the brothers. Lila, who is experiencing her first episode of 'dissolving margins', is horrified by what she sees. Rino is triumphant when the fireworks of the Solara brothers run out before their own. They then hear gunshots from the Solaras' balcony. Enzo immediately understands what is going on and pushes the girls inside. Rino is the last one outside, still hurling insults, and Lila runs back out to drag him away.

Chapter 23

Tensions run high in the Cerullo family and Lila begins to stay at home to help her mother instead of going to the shoe shop with her father and brother. On the day of Befana things come to a head when, without telling Lila, Rino places the handcrafted shoes in their father's stocking. Fernando throws the shoes at Rino and beats him. Rino punishes his sister for his disappointment by treating her like a slave.

Chapter 24

Elena brings to an end her short-lived relationship with Gino when he humiliates Alfonso by laughing at him in class. A few days later, Lila tells Elena she has received two declarations of love within a day. The first was from Pasquale, who Lila tried to let down gently by saying she could only love him like a brother. The second was from Marcello Solara, who abandoned his car in the middle of the street, pleaded forgiveness for his past behaviour and asked her to become engaged to him. In response, Lila called Marcello 'an animal' and vowed that she would never marry him. Elena advises Lila not to tell anyone about Marcello's declaration but later discovers that the news is already all around the neighborhood.

Chapter 25

At high school Professor Gerace enthusiastically praises a Greek paper Elena has written on the tragedy of Dido. Elena soon realises that Gerace has circulated the paper among the other members of staff, as other teachers sometimes stop to give her praise, including

25

Professor Galiani, a woman with an incisive mind who is well known to be a Communist. Galiani questions Elena about the main premise behind her paper and offers to lend her some books. Elena is aware that the ideas she developed in her paper were originally inspired by a conversation she had with Lila.

Still pining over Nino, Elena follows him on a couple of occasions but he still doesn't seem to recognise her. Meanwhile, Marcello continues his dogged pursuit of Lila.

Chapter 26

One Sunday Lila and Elena go into the city with Carmela, Pasquale and Rino. Although Rino and Pasquale are opposed to the idea, Lila insists that they go to Piazza Amedeo - an area favoured by the elegant and wealthy. On the way, the Solara brothers pass in their car, with Gigliola and Ada as passengers.

When they reach the piazza, Elena immediately realises that they are horribly out of place among the fashionable rich. To quell their uneasiness, the group begin to mock the clothes of the passers-by. When Rino goes too far and makes a vulgar comment to a passing couple, the well-dressed young man confronts Rino and calls him a 'hick'. Rino starts screaming abuse and punches the man until Lila intervenes, dragging him away. Rino and Pasquale instruct the girls to go home alone but they disobey and see Rino and Pasquale being chased and beaten by the well-dressed young man and a group of his friends. Lila tries to intervene and is knocked to the ground. The Solara brothers pull up in their car and Marcello helps Lila up before throwing himself into the fight. Michele then gets out of the car with an iron bar and joins in with a 'cold ferocity' that frightens Elena. Rino asks Marcello to take the girls away and they squeeze into the car with an annoyed Gigliola and Ada.

Chapter 27

At the end of the school term, while Gino fails and Alfonso has to retake a subject, Elena is promoted and receives a scholarship. At her father's insistence, Elena goes to see Maestra Oliviero with a gift of sugar and coffee to thank her for her help. Maestra Oliviero tells Elena that she has a cousin who lives on Ischia and will see if

26

Elena can stay with her for a well-earned holiday.

Elena resists the urge to flout her academic successes in front of Lila, as things are still not going well for her friend. After the fight in the piazza, Marcello visited the shoe shop to ask after Rino's health. A few days later, he returned with some shoes to repair and took Rino for a drive, offering to lend him his car for driving lessons. Lila is worried that the Solara brothers are seducing her brother and making a fool of him. One evening Rino unexpectedly brings Marcello home with him for dinner. During the meal Marcello flatters Fernando's skills as a shoemaker and then asks to see the pair of shoes made by Rino and Lila. When Fernando and Rino instruct Lila to fetch the shoes, she leaves the room and doesn't return. Rino and Fernando are furious. After Marcello leaves, Elena finds Lila sitting with the shoes in her lap. She tells Elena she doesn't want Marcello to touch them.

Chapter 28

Rino punishes his sister in the following days, often physically hurting her. They come to an uneasy truce when Rino persuades Lila that their father might change his mind about the project if Marcello likes the shoes. After Lila speaks to him Fernando agrees to display the shoes in the shop window on the understanding that, if someone wants to buy them, he may reconsider Rino's proposal. The shoes sit in the window for several weeks without anyone showing any interest. One day, however, Marcello comes into the shop and tells Fernando he wants to marry Lila.

Chapter 29

Rino reacts badly to this turn of events and falls ill with a fever. Fernando tells Lila that the future of her whole family lies in her answer to Marcello's proposal and advises her to consent on the understanding that there would be a long engagement. When Lila says she would rather drown herself, her father threatens to break every bone in her body.

One day Elena returns home to find Maestra Oliviero informing her mother that she has arranged for Elena to stay on Ischia until the end of August. When Maestra Oliviero leaves, Elena's mother is furious but, nevertheless, makes her daughter a

27

bathing suit and takes her to the ferry two days later. Elena is both terrified and happy at the prospect of leaving home for the first time.

Chapter 30

Maestra Oliviero's cousin, Nella Incardo, rents rooms to vacationers in Barano. While Elena stays with her she sleeps in the kitchen, makes breakfast for the guests and helps around the house. Otherwise she is free to do as she pleases. Disbelieving of her mother's claim that she taught her to swim at the beach when she was little, Elena is at first anxious about going in the sea. She quickly finds she can swim, however, and begins to feel a great sense of well-being. Lila's absence is the only thing that detracts from her pleasure. She writes to her friend but Lila doesn't reply.

Nella announces that Elena will soon have company of her own age, as a Neapolitan family with a seventeen-year-old son are coming to stay the following day. She adds that she keeps a book written by the father of the family on her bedside table and has learned the poems by heart. She shows Elena the book of poetry which is 'Attempts at Serenity' by Donato Sarratore. The dedication reads to 'darling Nella'.

Chapter 31

The next day Elena is disappointed when Donato and Lidia Sarratore arrive with every one of their children except for Nino. Nino's sister, Marisa, has heard all about Elena's successes at school from Nino. Elena is surprised, realising that Nino must have noticed her all along. Marisa tells Elena that Nino hates their father and will arrive on Ischia in three days' time when Donato has returned to work. During his stay on the island Donato makes himself very agreeable to all the women. They are all sorry when he leaves.

Chapter 32

Nino arrives but shows no emotion at finding Elena there. Although initially monosyllabic, he begins to talk to Elena about books. Completely besotted, Elena hangs on his every word and

28

even carries his things to the beach for him. One night Nino tells Elena that he always envied the friendship she shared with Lila. Reminding Elena that he once declared his love to her, he says that he imagined that they would get engaged and then all three of them would be together forever. Elena is hurt when Nino comments on how smart Lila was. After this point she stops writing letters to her friend.

Nino asks after Melina and expresses his disgust at the way his father seduced her, despite her vulnerability. After declaring that he will devote his life to not being like his father, he gives Elena a light kiss and tells her he is leaving the next day.

<u>Chapter 33</u>

Elena cries all night and runs to the port the next morning but Nino has already gone. In the guesthouse she finds a bookmark of Nino's and kisses it every night before she goes to sleep. In Nino's absence, Donato returns for a two-week holiday. In contrast to his son, he is a cheery presence. Elena is surprised to observe that the amateur poet never opens a book nor asks what she is reading. One day he reads an article aloud from *Roma*. After fishing for compliments about the article from Elena, he reveals that he wrote it.

<u>Chapter 34</u>

As Elena's fifteenth birthday falls while she is staying on Ischia, Nella and the Sarratore family insist on having a party to celebrate. At the same time, Elena receives a letter from Lila. In the letter Lila explains that she hasn't written before as she didn't want to spoil Elena's vacation. She goes on to say that, with her father's consent, Marcello now comes to dinner at her family's house every night. He has also presented them with a television which half the neighborhood come around to watch. While Rino has recovered from his fever, he ignores Marcello and is angry with his sister, feeling that she has abandoned him to his fate in the shoe shop. Her parents are also angry with her because she is rude to Marcello. Meanwhile, Marcello is devoted to her but says that he will kill her if she shows interest in any other man. Lila is scared and describes a frightening incident when a big copper pot exploded while she

29

was washing up. Lila says that she feels as if everything will break unless she can find a solution to her predicament. Elena feels great sympathy for Lila but is also envious of the quality of her friend's writing style.

Chapter 35

Elena tells her companions that she may have to leave the next day as a friend of hers is in trouble. As she lies awake in her bed in the kitchen, Donato enters the room and urges her to stay. Without any encouragement he kisses and caresses her. Elena remains immobile, feeling both horror and pleasure. Donato says that he loves her and he knows that she loves him. First thing in the morning, Elena leaves a note for Nella and leaves. She knows that her feelings of disgust and shame will prevent her from telling Lila what has happened.

Chapter 36

When Elena returns home, Lila is delighted to see her. She takes her to the grocery store, which has expanded, and shows her Stefano's expensive sports car which is far more luxurious than the one owned by the Solara brothers. Stefano tells Elena that he bought the car for Lila hoping that she would ride in it at least once. Both girls get in the car with Stefano and Elena is aware that, by doing so, Lila is setting a significant chain of events in motion. Stefano asks Lila if the shoes in the window of her father's shop are the ones that she made. When he compliments them, Lila tells him to buy them. He drives straight to the shoemaker's shop.

Chapter 37

Stefano is courteous to Lila's brother and father and tries on the handmade shoes. Although the they are tight, he says he will take them after the leather has been stretched. He also asks about their plans to make similar shoes and, when he sees Lila's designs, asks if he can borrow them. When they leave, Lila accuses Stefano of treating her family like fools and tells him that it is not possible to buy her. Stefano argues that he is a businessman and he sees real potential in the shoes. Elena feels that the two have come to an unspoken agreement.

Chapter 38

Lila starts to frequently visit Stefano's grocery store with Elena as a chaperone. She explains to Elena that she intends to get rid of Marcello through Stefano.

Stefano pays 25,000 lire for the handmade shoes and another 20,000 lire for Lila's designs, which he says he wants to frame. Shortly afterwards, he rents the space adjacent to the shoe shop and tells the Cerullo family that it is at their disposal if they ever want to expand. They come to an agreement that Stefano will pay the expenses and they will start to produce exact copies of Lila's designs. Any profits from 'Cerullo shoes' will be split equally.

Marcello continues to visit Lila's family in the evening but finds he is less enthusiastically received by Fernando and Nunzia.

Chapter 39

Stefano has Lila's designs framed and asks Fernando's permission to hang them on the walls of the shoe shop. He then announces that he wants to marry Lila. When Fernando tells him that Lila is already engaged to Marcello, Stefano asks him to let his daughter decide who she wishes to marry. They call Lila in and she agrees to marry Stefano. Fernando points out that they will be offending the entire Solara family. Lila says that she will break the news to Marcello herself.

Chapter 40

Two days later, when Marcello arrives for dinner, Lila asks him to take her out for an ice cream. As soon as they are outside, Lila coldly tells him that she loves Stefano. Marcello announces that he would kill her if he didn't love her so much and rushes off, devastated.

Chapter 41

Lila is pleased with the way things have turned out. While the shoe project provides opportunities for her family, she has also got rid of Marcello and is engaged to a respectable and wealthy man.

When school begins again Elena studies hard and becomes good friends with Stefano's younger brother, Alfonso. Gino is jealous and begins to spread rumours about Elena. Despite still loving Nino, Elena has avoided him since she returned from Ischia as she is overwhelmed with disgust at what happened with his father. She feels the need to catch up with Lila and get herself a fiancé worthy of envy.

Chapter 42

Elena starts to feel unattractive again as her tan fades and her acne returns. One day, in class, Professor Gerace realises that Elena can't see the blackboard properly and insists that her parents must take her to an oculist. The oculist diagnoses severe myopia and Elena has to resign herself to wearing spectacles, which make her feel even less attractive. After leaving her spectacles behind in the classroom one day, Elena is heart-broken when she goes back for them to find that they are broken. She cries as she knows her parents will be furious at the unnecessary cost. Lila tells Elena to leave the spectacles with her and returns with them a few days later. Stefano has paid for them to be fixed by an optician.

Chapter 43

Lila continually shows off the gifts that Stefano has given her and shows no interest in Elena's studies. Elena tries to convince herself that, while Lila has Stefano, her own 'wealth' lies in her education: a privilege that Lila has lost. Elena becomes preoccupied with the idea that there must be a hierarchy within the Holy Trinity. She tries to talk to Lila about it, who dismisses her concerns as trivial.

Chapter 44

Lila is both resented and admired for the fine clothes she has started to wear, which seem to elevate her above the poverty of the neighborhood. Elena observes that she has also learned to enhance and show off her beauty. Meanwhile, Stefano seems to view Lila as the embodiment of his future success and prosperity.

32

Chapter 45

Elena spends less and less time with Lila. Meanwhile, Pasquale is evidently finding it difficult to see Lila with Stefano. One day Pasquale criticises Lila, pointing out that the money she has encouraged Stefano to invest in the shoe store has come from Don Achille's ill-gotten gains. Enzo jumps to Lila's defence and their friends just manage to stop the incident exploding into violence.

Chapter 46

Tensions run high in the shoe shop as Fernando suggests that Lila's shoe designs are impractical, while Stefano quietly insists that they be made to exactly replicate her designs. Fernando and Rino are often heard quarrelling. Lila, on the other hand, appears entirely content with her role as the future wife of Stefano and seems to have become sweeter natured.

One day Elena discovers that Marcello has been bragging that Lila regularly gave him a 'blow job' when he visited her house. Although Elena doesn't even understand what this means, she hopes that the rumours don't reach Stefano. Eventually Elena decides to tell Lila about the gossip and is astonished to discover that her friend already knows. Lila pronounces the rumours to be false and says the prospect of the act is so disgusting she would never perform it on any man. She adds that Stefano has also heard the rumours and they have taken the joint decision to rise above them. Elena observes that taking the moral high ground in this way is unprecedented in the neighborhood. She wonders if Lila intends to transform the culture of the neighborhood singlehandedly.

Chapter 47

Despite Lila's decision to rise above Marcello's lies, Pasquale and the other neighborhood boys still feel they need to take revenge on her behalf. The next day Elena discovers that the Solara brothers have been savagely beaten and their car has been destroyed. The brothers claim that they were attacked on a dark street by at least ten men. Elena realises that there were only three attackers; Pasquale, Enzo and Antonio. She expects to hear that the Solara brothers have taken some sort of revenge but nothing more

33

happens.

While Elena is taking her exams in the second year of high school, Lila tells her that she will be getting married in the spring when she will be just sixteen-and-a-half.

Chapter 48

The news of Lila's imminent wedding upsets Elena and she secretly hopes that something will happen to make Stefano break off the engagement. Schoolwork suddenly seems meaningless to her and she stops revising for her exams.

Despite her lack of application to her studies, Elena is promoted to the third year with all tens. One of her papers is highly praised by her teachers and Elena realises that she has been trying to adopt Lila's fluid writing style and evidently succeeded.

On her father's instructions, Elena goes to visit Maestra Oliviero to get the books for the following year in advance. Maestra Oliviero, who is noticeably unwell, begins to talk about Lila, who she has seen from a distance in the street with her fiancé. Elena is shocked when Maestra Oliviero declares that Lila's 'beauty of mind' has been wasted, ending up only 'in her face, in her breasts, in her thighs, in her ass'. Secretly, however, Elena is also pleased to be thought of as the only successful student.

Elena scouts around for a job over the summer. She is pleased when the woman who runs the stationers asks if she would take her three girls swimming during the holidays. Afterwards she bumps into Melina's son, Antonio Cappuccio, who is now a mechanic. When Antonio asks Elena if she will be his girlfriend, she says yes even though she still loves Nino.

Chapter 49

Every day Elena travels across the city with the stationer's three daughters to a beach called the Sea Garden. In the evenings she sees Antonio and they go to a part of the neighborhood known as the ponds. Assuming that this is the kind of thing Lila does with Stefano, Elena allows Antonio to touch her intimately and does the same to him.

One day when Elena is at the beach with the children and Antonio, they see Lila and Stefano there. Lila asks if Elena loves

34

Antonio and she admits that she doesn't. Lila, on the other hand, says she loves Stefano more than anyone except Elena.

Chapter 50

In light of her conversation with Lila, Elena feels she should break it off with Antonio but can't bring herself to do it. Antonio is worried about the mental health of his mother, who keeps insisting that she has seen Donato Sarratore. Secretly Elena worries that Melina might be telling the truth as she still has nightmares about Nino's father.

One morning Elena's fears are realised when Donato Sarratore stops her in the street. He tells her that he thinks of her constantly and has written a poem about her. Elena tells him that she has a boyfriend but Donato insists that he will wait at the entrance to the tunnel on the *stradone* every day at noon. He tries to kiss her and she jumps away in disgust.

That evening Elena tells Antonio that she bumped into Donato. She claims he asked her to tell Melina that he would wait at the tunnel entrance for her every day. Elena suggests that they both go to meet Donato to warn him about the state of Melina's health.

The next day Elena and Antonio go to the tunnel together and find Donato waiting there. Antonio thanks Donato for all the help he gave his family but says that if his mother sees him even once more she will end up in an asylum. Donato objects to staying away from the neighborhood but Antonio threatens him and he backs down. Antonio starts shaking after the encounter and Elena realises what a burden has fallen on him since the death of his father and the collapse of his mother. She resolves to leave him after Lila's wedding.

Chapter 51

Lila takes Elena to see her luxurious apartment in the new neighborhood, which has a huge bathtub and a view of Vesuvius. As further proof of her happiness Lila tells her about an incident where Stefano demonstrated his love for her when he became emotional about the first pair of shoes that she designed and helped to make. Elena asks Lila what she and Stefano do when they are alone together. Lila replies that, as they are not yet married,

35

they just kiss. Elena struggles to equate this information with the freedom that Lila seems to enjoy. She is too ashamed to admit that she has gone much further than this with Antonio.

Chapter 52

Stefano's sister, Pinuccia, becomes angry at the preferential treatment Lila receives. She announces that if her future sister-in-law does not start to help in the grocery store, she will also refuse to work there. To appease his sister, Stefano suggests that Pinuccia and his mother help with the wedding preparations and gets Ada Cappuccio to replace them in the store.

The involvement of her future in-laws in her plans irritates Lila and she persuades Elena to support her decision making. When they go to look at wedding dresses, Lila and her future in-laws disagree for hours on which style to choose. Lila finally calls on Elena to settle the argument, who gives a conciliatory speech suggesting a style that incorporates the favourite elements on both sides. Both parties happily agree to her suggestion. Afterwards Lila points out that, while people are generally afraid of her, Elena is good at making herself liked.

Chapter 53

From this point Elena is constantly called on to arbitrate in discussions about the wedding. As a result, she neglects her studies and even misses a few school sessions. For the first time, she receives a less than brilliant report card and barely passes in some subjects.

Elena has noticed that her religious education teacher constantly criticises the communists for their atheism. She feels compelled to react, particularly as her favourite teacher is the communist Professor Galiani. One day Elena suggests that it is foolish to trust in the existence of God when human existence is quite obviously governed by 'the blind fury of chance' and the religious education teacher sends her out of the classroom. Elena begins to cry, struggling to understand why she has done something so reckless. She then realises that she was articulating one of Lila's opinions. Nino approaches her in the corridor and, when she tells him what has happened, he goes to fetch Professor

36

Galiani. After lavishly praising Elena, Galiani goes into the religious education class. Five minutes later, she emerges to say that Elena can go back in as long as she apologises to the Professor for her aggressive tone. The incident soon makes Elena a 'heroine' among her friends and a certain group of teachers. She also tries to make herself as agreeable to the teachers she has offended as possible, thus keeping both camps happy.

Nino asks Elena to write an account of her conflict with the religious education teacher for a journal he contributes to. He explains that he has described the incident to the editors, who have said that they would try to publish the account in the next issue. Elena writes the article and consults with Lila on the final result. Lila makes some changes but then declares that she doesn't want to read anything else that Elena writes as it is painful for her.

Chapter 54

Elena realises that the changes Lila has made to her article have improved it. The next day she gives it to Nino. After reading her article, Nino sadly admits that Elena is a better writer than him. He walks off without saying goodbye and, for a moment, Elena sees 'his father's gait' in his stride. Soon afterwards, Elena asks Antonio to come and pick her up from school and, for Nino's benefit, makes a public show of affection for him.

Chapter 55

Feeling that she will need his support, Elena asks Antonio to accompany her to Lila's wedding and tells him not to leave her alone at any point during the day. Assuming that Elena wants to make their relationship official, Antonio gets into debt by buying a new suit for the occasion.

Meanwhile, Rino and Fernando summon Stefano to show him the shoes that they have made. Stefano is critical of any modifications made to the original designs but Lila is delighted with them and argues that the modifications are minor and probably necessary. The elegant shoes appear in the window at Christmas.

37

Chapter 56

Lila is increasingly concerned about Rino. Disappointed that the new shoes haven't sold immediately, he has become depressed and often flies into rages.

One day Lila asks Elena to accompany her to see Maestra Oliviero as she wants to deliver a wedding invitation in person. When they arrive at her house, however, Maestra Oliviero claims not to recognise Lila and shuts the door in her face.

Stefano changes his mind over who is to be speech master at the wedding, telling Lila that he has replaced their original choice with Silvio Solara. Lila is furious and refuses to speak to him. Stefano asks Rino to explain to his sister that Silvio Solara is an important contact for placing Cerullo shoes in desirable shops. Rino accuses Lila of putting everything he has worked for in jeopardy but she still does not come round. Eventually, Lila's mother visits Elena and asks her to speak to her daughter. Elena does so, pointing out that Lila is confusing Stefano with the Solara brothers, who will have no importance in her future life. Lila finally relents on the condition that Marcello Solara must not set foot at her wedding.

Chapter 57

The day of the wedding arrives and Elena goes to help Lila get ready at her old house. Lila is still preoccupied with the way Maestra Oliviero snubbed her. Revealing her trepidation about her own future, Lila tells Elena that she must continue studying so that she will always be her 'brilliant friend'.

As Elena helps Lila to bathe, she sees her friend naked for the first time. She feels many conflicting emotions, including a pleasure at seeing her beautiful body before Stefano possesses it.

Chapter 58

The church wedding service goes smoothly. Towards the end, Elena spots Nino standing at the back.

38

Chapter 59

Disquieted by seeing Nino, Elena travels in a car to the reception with her old friends. For the first time she is struck by the violent language of the boys and realises that, although she grew up with them, she is no longer one of them.

Chapter 60

At the wedding reception the friends that Elena has grown up with have paired off into couples: Rino with Pinuccia; Pasquale with Ada; Enzo with Carmela, and Alfonso with Marisa. Elena's mother is angry when she sees her daughter with Antonio, stating she hasn't sent her to school to ruin herself with a mechanic. While her mother instructs her to sit close to her, Antonio wants Elena to sit with him. When she sees Nino enter the room, she ignores both of them and goes over to him.

Chapter 61

Elena sits at a table with Nino, Alfonso and Marisa. Antonio comes over to say he has kept a place for her but Elena dismisses him, saying that her mother is angry and suspicious. Intimidated, he returns to his table. Encouraging Nino to tell her about his latest article, Elena avoids looking at Antonio and resolves to break it off with him the next day. Dazzled by Nino, she believes that he is the one who will help her escape the neighborhood.

Antonio complains that he has bought a new suit, only to sit and watch Elena talking to a scruffy youth who isn't even wearing a tie. He storms outside onto the terrace. Elena goes back to Nino and asks him when the magazine will come out with her article in it. He tells her that the magazine came out a couple of weeks ago but they didn't have room to put her piece in.

Chapter 62

Elena tries to hide her intense disappointment, realising that she had thought of the publication of her article as her first step towards a different kind of 'destiny'. She recalls Maestra Oliviero's reference to 'the plebs' and associates it with the drunkenness, quarrelling, and vulgar toasts she witnesses around her. Nino leaves the reception with barely a goodbye.

As the wedding cake is presented, the Solara brothers appear at the reception. Elena sees Lila turn pale as she looks at Marcello's feet. He is wearing the first pair of shoes that Lila and Rino made together, initially bought by Stefano.

LITERARY STYLE

Elena Ferrante's novels tend to evoke one of two reactions in readers: effusive appreciation or intense dislike. This divergence of opinion is largely down to Ferrante's tone which is almost unrelentingly dark and angry. Those looking for uplifting fiction will certainly not find it in Ferrante's fiction. What they will find is a brutal honesty and raw energy that is unique to the author.

Ferrante's unique tone stems largely from her extraordinary use of language. The author has commented in interview that, 'Writing for me is a dragnet that carries everything along with it'. This idea neatly summarises Ferrante's style. Her sentences, which often run into one another and build with dizzying momentum, seem to flow with an energy of their own, leading some critics to compare her writing to a volcanic eruption. The feverish intensity of these outpourings reflect the state of mind of her conflicted characters. Readers can do little else but give in and be swept along by the tide of Ferrante's prose and immerse themselves in the interior world of her characters. The overall impression in *My Brilliant Friend* is that Elena's narrative is driven by an uncontrollable flow of emotion, contributing to the novel's confessional, autobiographical feel.

Ferrante adds to the sense that Elena's narrative is an autobiographical outpouring through the novel's non-linear structure. Her account, triggered by memories, casts backwards and forwards to trace the source of key events. Elena describes certain incidents (such as the episode with the dolls in the cellar and she and Lila's visit to Don Achille) and then abandons them, only later returning to describe the consequences of what took place. Similarly, she also provides tantalising glimpses of what is to happen in the future, beyond the confines of the novel. When describing Lila's first episode of 'dissolving margins', for instance, she explains that, although the incident took place in 1958 on New Year's Eve, Lila didn't tell her about it until 1980 when they were

41

both thirty-six-year-old wives with children of their own. This non-linear structure also contributes to the sense we get in Ferrante's novels that life is too chaotic an experience to neatly order within tidy sentence structures or strictly chronological narratives.

Unsurprisingly, *My Brilliant Friend* also defies any kind of neat genre categorisation. A number of critics have compared Ferrante's Neapolitan quartet to the series of books written by the Norwegian author Karl Ove Knausgaard. Titled 'My Struggle', Knausgaard's six autobiographical novels were published between 2009 and 2011 and became bestsellers when translated into English. Like Knausgaard's novels, Ferrante's Neapolitan series plays with the divide between fiction and autobiography. By deliberately concealing her own identity, Ferrante blurs the distinction between fact and fiction even further, leaving readers to wildly speculate on how much of her subject matter is autobiographical.

Ferrante's Neapolitan quartet can also be viewed in the context of classic domestic fiction. In an introduction to *Sense and Sensibility* Ferrante points out that Jane Austen 'rests a clear gaze on the condition of women' and warns the reader to 'pay attention, for the lightness conceals pitiless depths - it's a gaze that, miraculously, doesn't sweeten anything.' This assessment of Austen's work could just as easily be applied to Ferrante's own novels which, although lacking Austen's lightness of tone, dissect the frustrations and limitations of women's lives with an intelligent and mercilessly frank gaze. *My Brilliant Friend* also has much in common with classic bildungsroman or coming-of-age tales, such as *Jane Eyre*, in which the protagonist grows up during the course of the novel, suffers a number of trials and passes from innocence to experience.

While influenced by domestic fiction and the bildungsroman, however, Ferrante's novels sometimes break away from the realist style associated with both of these genres. As Meghan O'Rourke points out in a review of the Neapolitan novels in *The Guardian*, 'a hallmark of Ferrante's writing is this juxtaposition between matter-of-factness and metaphor, between hyperrealism and hallucinatory distortion'. While *My Brilliant Friend* is recognisably set in the real world, the narrative often takes on a nightmarish quality. It also sometimes has the feel of a fable or fairy tale, as Ferrante invests certain everyday objects (a silver bracelet, a copper pot, a pair of shoes) with symbolic significance.

Another interesting influence in *My Brilliant Friend* is classical

42

literature. Critic Rachel Donadio points out that Elena Greco literally means Helen the Greek, and the learning of classical languages plays an important part in the competitive battle between Elena and Lila. Significantly, Lila is fascinated by *The Aeneid* and identifies particularly with the character of Dido. In Greek mythology, Dido was the founder and Queen of Carthage who, rather than allowing herself to be blackmailed into accepting an unwelcome marriage proposal, throws herself into the flames of a funeral pyre. Dido's fate has obvious parallels with the Hobson's choice Lila is faced with when Marcello Solara proposes to her. Lila's decision to marry Stefano instead is a less tragic solution than the one Dido comes up with but, nevertheless, emphasises the limited options open to her as a woman. One of many references to Greek tragedy in the novel, it highlights the struggles of not only Lila, but all the female characters, in trying to avoid the inevitable fate that destiny seems to have laid out for them.

HISTORICAL CONTEXT: ITALY & NAPLES

Ferrante's Naples

Ferrante's Neapolitan novels span a period of Italian history from the 1950s to the present day. Beginning with the Italian post-war economic slump in *My Brilliant Friend*, the novels that follow go on to describe the changing face of Italy, including its economic boom of the 1960s and the political turbulence of the 1970s.

In *My Brilliant Friend*, Ferrante powerfully evokes both the landscape and the atmosphere of Naples. If readers are hoping for an elegy on the beauty of Italian landscape and architecture, however, they will be disappointed. In Ferrante's novel, Naples (particularly the area on the outskirts where Elena lives known as the neighborhood) is an ugly combination of oppressive heat, dusty streets, disorder and violence. With an angry character to match those of its inhabitants, the volatile nature of the city is symbolised by the presence of Mount Vesuvius looming over it.

Although Ferrante makes it clear that Naples holds some charms, such as the beauty of the sea and the wealthier areas of the city, her characters are unable to access them – symbolised in the unsuccessful excursion Elena and Lila make to reach the sea and the violent confrontation they witness when they venture into the wealthy area of Naples. The explosive nature of the Naples neighborhood is embodied in the Bar Solara, where the owner keeps a stick behind the bar for customers who fail to pay. It is in this bar that many local men suffer gambling losses and reach the point of '*desperazione*'. The men then return home to their families and vent their frustration by beating their wives and children.

As well as portraying the atmosphere of the neighborhood in Naples, Ferrante offers telling glimpses into the corrupt politics and economics that lie behind it. While Elena and Lila imagine Don Achille as an ogre with a black loot bag it soon becomes clear

44

to the reader that he is a feared member of the Camorra (the Neapolitan version of the Mafia) who has made his money from the black market. Meanwhile, the Bar Solara is not only the scene of drunken brawls but also the favoured hangout for those involved in organised crime including loan sharks from the Camorra, smugglers and corrupt politicians. The prosperity of the Carracci and the Solara family, who dominate the neighborhood, have their foundations in corruption. Ferrante suggests that the corrupt nature of the neighborhood is a microcosm of the wider corruption of Italy as a whole.

Elena's narrative also draws attention to the historical changes taking place within Italian society. When she and Lila find a gas mask in a cellar it is a reminder of a history that they are not fully aware of: the sustained bombing of Naples during the Second World War. Elena also glimpses the beginnings of Italy's economic boom as she notices that small businesses have begun to flourish in the neighborhood. Lila's sudden improvement in lifestyle when she becomes engaged to Stefano is a tangible example of the possibilities of upward mobility.

The History of Naples

While Naples has a long and varied history, the aspects which are relevant to Ferrante's novel begin with the Second World War. During World War II Naples was occupied by the Germans and, due to its status as a port, became a strategic bombing target for Allied forces. In 1943, when the Nazis evacuated the city, they destroyed the whole port. When Allied troops arrived, they were faced with trying to restore the city's water, gas and electricity systems, which had all been destroyed by the Germans. To make matters worse, in 1944 the city was further devastated by an eruption from Mount Vesuvius.

Although Naples had already been a poor city, the impact of the war made it worse. While the wealthy fled to areas such as Sorrento or Capri, the poor were left behind to make the best of things. Of those who remained, only those trading in the black market (goods imported by and stolen from the Allies) benefited. As a result, criminal organisations such as the Camorra began to flourish. The majority of Neapolitans, however, remained poor and uneducated and this lack of education was reflected in their use of language.

45

While the rest of Italy largely spoke proper Italian, less educated Neapolitans would generally speak only in Neapolitan dialect. This meant that their lack of education led to difficulties in communicating with the rest of the world.

Another significant struggle taking place in Italy during this period was the conflict between Italian Fascism and Communism. From 1922 to 1945, Italy was governed by the Fascist Party, first under Benito Mussolini (who allied Italy with Nazi Germany in WWII) and then by the Republican Fascist Party. Italian Fascism sought to restore the country to its former glory by expanding Italian territories. Opposed to liberalism, the movement was also anti-feminist, reinforcing traditional gender roles. Mussolini perceived women's primary role to be childbearing and the Italian Fascist government offered financial incentives to women who raised large families, while bringing in policies to reduce the number of women in employment. In direct opposition to Italian Fascism was the Italian Communist Party, founded in 1921. Outlawed by the Fascist government, the Communist Party played a major part in the Italian resistance movement during the war. After the Second World War it became the second largest political party of Italy, making it the largest communist party in the West.

The history of Naples as a city entrenched in poverty, corruption and violence continues even today. Unemployment remains high, there is a thriving black market and organised crime remains deeply rooted in Neapolitan culture.

THEMES & IMAGERY

THEMES

Friendship

One of the most remarkable aspects of *My Brilliant Friend* is its portrayal of female friendship. Elena and Lila's enduring relationship is the glue that binds all of the Neapolitan novels together. While they remain bound together through the years, their feelings for each other are not always amiable or supportive. Within their complex friendship there are moments of real solidarity but also seething resentments.

When they first meet, Elena and Lila are the antithesis of each other in looks and temperament. Elena is fair, healthily rounded and eager to please, while Lila is dark, skinny and hostile. This obvious contrast between the two girls goes on to be reflected in their experiences. As if on a see-saw, the girls' fortunes seem to rise and fall in direct opposition to each other. Whenever Elena feels her life has taken a turn for the better, Lila suffers a setback, and vice versa.

Significantly, the friendship of the girls is sealed when they exchange dolls and, after Lila throws Elena's doll down the grate, Elena does the same with Lila's. This incident sets the tone for their lifelong relationship. Continually competing with each other, the girls engage in a struggle for supremacy in which the balance of power is always shifting. While Lila generally sets the pace, Elena is determined to keep up with her and even surpass her. This competitive attitude applies not only to tests of courage but also to educational achievements and their first sexual experiences.

47

While Elena and Lila always seek each other out, they often treat each other appallingly. Lila often rides roughshod over her friend's feelings and Elena cannot resist rubbing salt into Lila's wounds when she is unable to join her at middle school. This ongoing tension in their relationship is highlighted in the incident where Lila convinces Elena to bunk off school, only to abort their mission to reach the sea before they get there. Annoyed at being punished without even meeting their objective, Elena wonders whether Lila planned the excursion in the hope that Elena's parents would be so angry they would prevent her from going to middle school. With the benefit of hindsight, however, Elena comes to the conclusion that Lila both did and did not want this to happen. This sums up the girls' conflicting feelings in which they simultaneously wish each other both good and ill. Even Elena's decision to write about Lila seems to both a mark of her affection and an act of revenge, as it opposes Lila's evident wish to erase herself from the world.

While this complicated relationship sometimes borders on the toxic, Ferrante makes it clear that the girls need each other. When Elena starts middle school she is initially pleased that Lila isn't there to outshine her. She quickly discovers, however, that in Lila's absence, she lacks the motivation to push herself. Without Lila there to observe her achievements or failures, she lacks a sense of purpose. In this way, Ferrante highlights the symbiotic nature of their relationship. Elena, in particular, gains a sense of identity only by comparing and contrasting herself to Lila. There are also moments in the novel when the girls show great empathy and solidarity with each other. Lila's reluctance to spoil Elena's vacation in Ischia by writing with her bad news is surprisingly thoughtful and Elena is sympathetic to her friend's plight. Similarly, Lila's instruction to Elena to continue studying and become her 'brilliant friend' is also a genuine expression that she will go on to great things on behalf of them both.

The relationship between Elena and Lila is so intense that it often resembles a romance or marriage rather than a friendship. The possessiveness they feel for each other isn't just apparent in their petty jealousy over friendships with other girls. While her friend is known as Lina to everyone else, it is only Elena who calls her Lila. By giving her this pet name, Elena suggests that she feels a sense of ownership and intimacy with Lila that the rest of the world is excluded from. On another occasion Lila's possessiveness over Elena is illustrated when she fiercely defends her honour by threatening the Solara brothers with a knife. Lila's instinct to protect her friend from the brothers' sexual advances is a reaction more typical of a lover than a friend. The sexual undercurrent in the girls' relationship comes to a head when Elena helps Lila to bathe on her wedding day. On seeing her friend naked for the first time, Elena feels great agitation. She also takes some pleasure in the fact that she is seeing Lila's body before Stefano. Her idea that Stefano will despoil Lila with his touch unconsciously articulates her fear that he will also replace her in Lila's affections. Lila makes it clear, however, that her love for Stefano doesn't surpass the fierce love she feels for her friend.

Violence

From early on in their childhoods Elena and Lila become accustomed to violence as a part of everyday life. The neighborhood is an explosive mix of poverty and illegal activity which regularly erupts both in the privacy of the home and in public. Elena notes that much of the conflict in her own home arises from their lack of money while, at the Bar Solara, where the owner wields a stick for anyone who doesn't pay, trouble often erupts when gambling customers reach 'the point of *desperazione* - a word that in dialect meant having lost all hope but also being broke'. When Don Achille, the neighborhood loan shark, is gruesomely murdered in his own home, it is assumed that the accused murderer, Alfredo Peluso, has reached exactly this point of *desperazione*. The mood of building violence that pervades the neighborhood is beautifully illustrated in the battle of fireworks at Stefano's New Year's Eve party. Ferrante captures the increasingly frenzied atmosphere as the young men, led by Rino, light fireworks until the Solara brothers start firing guns at the party. The overwhelming sense of aggression in the air causes Elena to remember, years later, 'the swirl of males whose bodies gave off a heat hotter than the fires in the sky'.

Elena describes how the neighborhood men turn their feelings of impotence and frustration on their families. In this setting, girls and women take it for granted that they will beaten by their fathers or husbands if they step out of line. This is graphically illustrated when Lila's father throws his ten-year-old daughter out of the window, breaking her arm, after she insults him. Similarly, when the Solara brothers try to coax Elena into their car, she is largely deterred by the certainty her father 'would beat her to death' if he found out, while her little brothers would feel obligated to try to take revenge on the Solara brothers. The repayment of dishonourable behaviour towards a sister with violence is an unspoken rule in the neighborhood.

Nevertheless, violence is by no means the sole preserve of men in the novel. Elena notes that women frequently attack each other and describes a particularly disturbing incident where Melina and Lidia Sarratorre roll down the stairs as they fight until Melina's head hits the floor. Suggesting that there is a special quality to the anger that fuels female violence, Elena imagines that 'tiny animals' infect the water and air of the neighborhood, making its women, 'as angry as starving dogs.' Elena believes that the women are, 'more severely infected than the men, because while men were always getting furious, they calmed down in the end; women, who appeared to be silent, acquiescent, when they were angry flew into a rage that had no end.' The notion that the repressed anger of a woman is more dangerous than that of a man is echoed in Lila's certainty that the murderer of Don Achille is a woman.

In many ways Lila epitomises female rage and violence. In contrast to Elena, whose natural impulse is to appease others, Lila seems to look for conflict in everything around her. She does not hesitate in retaliating when the boys at school throw rocks at her and inflicts a nasty gash on Enzo before being floored by a flying rock to the head. She also shows her unflinching capacity for violence when she holds a knife to Marcello's throat until she begins to draw blood. Interestingly, rather than making her less attractive, Lila's violent streak seems to provoke devotion in the opposite sex. Enzo presents Lila with a garland of sorb apples following the rock fight and, after this point, becomes her ardent defender. After Lila threatens him with a knife, Marcello becomes similarly besotted and becomes determined to make her his wife. The link between Lila, violence and sexual desire is also emphasised in the scene where Stefano confronts Lila after she outperforms his younger brother in the classroom. His threat to prick her tongue with a pin is both graphically unpleasant and strangely intimate. With this in mind, the fact that he becomes yet

50

another suitor of Lila's should not be a surprise.

As well as harbouring violent tendencies, Lila is also a catalyst for violence in the novel. As she hits puberty, Lila becomes the focus of many testosterone-fuelled conflicts between the young men of the neighborhood, from verbal insults to blows. Significantly, it is Lila's idea that she and her friends visit the Piazza Amedeo, where they all feel uncomfortably out of place and the boys consequently get into a nasty brawl with a wealthy group of young men. It is also Lila's effect on the opposite sex that leads her brother into several ugly confrontations and almost causes a fight at a party.

Interestingly, despite the many associations made between Lila and violence, towards the end of the novel she seems to genuinely desire to make the neighborhood a less violent place to live. Somewhat naively, Lila sees Stefano's open invitation to his New Year's Eve party as an attempt to heal the rift between feuding families. Later, when Marcello spreads lies about the sexual favours he supposedly enjoyed from her, Lila tells an astonished Elena that she and Stefano intend to set an example by rising above the malicious rumours. Any hopes Lila has of bringing peace to the neighborhood seem to be dashed, however, when Pasquale and the other neighborhood boys take revenge on her behalf by savagely beating the Solara brothers and destroying their car.

Women & Gender Roles

In a review of the Neapolitan quartet Joan Frank suggests that the novels are, 'one long, mind-and-heart-shredding howl for the history of women'. Ferrante's frustration with the restrictions of gender roles is evident throughout *My Brilliant Friend*, as Elena's narrative highlights the way she, and other women, are shaped by society's expectations.

As young girls, Elena and Lila are blissfully unaware that their gender may place restrictions on their aspirations. Fearlessly competing with the boys at school, they dream of becoming wealthy writers when they are older. When the girls decide to use the money Don Achille gives them for replacement dolls to buy a copy of *Little Women* instead, this is a sign that they have unconsciously rejected the traditional role of motherhood in favour of education. As Elena's narrative progresses, however, there is an

51

increasing awareness that their horizons are likely to be limited by society's expectations. Despite Lila's extraordinary intelligence, her dreams of continuing with her education come to an end when her father flings her out of a window. Meanwhile, while Elena manages to persuade her parents to allow her to continue in school, she becomes increasingly uneasy about the physical changes that puberty brings. When her burgeoning breasts attract unwelcome attention from her male classmates, Elena feels both shame and confusion as she realises she is the focus of sexual objectification.

Significantly, Elena's anxiety over the changes to her body are inextricably linked to her ambivalent feelings about her mother. Elena admits to feelings of repulsion for her mother which centre around her mother's crossed-eye and her limp. Unconsciously Elena equates her mother's physical flaws with motherhood. Dimly aware that her mother (who is incidentally only thirty-five by the end of the novel) was once an attractive young woman, Elena sees these physical imperfections as the result of a life given up to marriage and childbearing (a viewpoint echoed in her belief that Stefano will 'disfigure' Lila by getting her pregnant). Elena's fear that the changes in her body will continue until she finds herself transformed into her mother expresses her anxiety that womanhood will trap her into a lifetime of domestic drudgery and child-rearing. A pre-pubescent Lila expresses a similar feeling when Gigliola insults her by pointing out that none of the boys are sexually interested in her. When Lila enigmatically replies, 'It's better that way', it reflects her understanding that sexuality can be a poisoned chalice. Maestra Oliviero makes the same point in a different way when she declares that Lila's 'beauty of mind' has been wasted, ending up only 'in her face, in her breasts, in her thighs, in her ass'. While Elena is shocked at her former teacher's crude comment, Maestra Oliviero is mourning the way women's identities can be eclipsed so easily. Lila, once known for her brilliant mind, has become only an object of desire. As a result, her earlier dream of becoming rich by writing books has faded into acquiring wealth through marriage.

While *My Brilliant Friend* focuses largely on the teenage preoccupations of Elena and Lila, a cast of women in all stages of life parade in the background. While a handful, such as Professor Galiani and Maestra Oliviero, have achieved a different sort of life through education, the majority of the older women are noticeably beaten down by household chores, poverty, child-rearing and abusive husbands. Interestingly, Lila seems to grasp the full extent of female suffering much earlier than Elena. Her empathy with mad Melina demonstrates that she can easily understand how a woman's circumstances can destroy her sanity. Meanwhile, her confident assertion that the murderer of Don Achille must have been a woman indicates that she understands the ferocity of the anger simmering within many of the women of the neighborhood.

Class

The hurdles that Elena and Lila face in life are as much about class as gender. While Naples, as a whole, suffers from poverty, the neighborhood where the girls grow up is one of the least salubrious areas in the city. Lack of money lies at the heart of most domestic conflicts and gives the neighborhood its angry, volatile character.

Elena and Lila do not fully appreciate the chasm between the very poor and the very rich until their ill-fated visit to Piazza Amedeo. The 'humiliating difference' the group of teenagers feel between themselves and the upper-middle class people they see there leads to a vicious fight between the boys and a group of wealthy young men. Even before this point, however, Elena and Lila are conscious that money and social class make a difference to how the world treats you. When Marcello and Michele Solara treat Ada with disrespect by dragging her into their car, Lila points out that the brothers only felt entitled to do so because Ada comes from one of the poorest families in the neighborhood. Understanding that money brings power, Lila argues that she and Elena must make more money than the Solara family to make sure that they escape such treatment.

While both girls desperately want to rise above their class origins, the opportunities to do so are limited. Their families object to them continuing with their studies, not only because they are girls, but also because they can ill-afford to continue to support them. Of the two, Elena is the luckiest and class consciousness in some ways plays a part in her good fortune. While her mother is completely opposed to Elena continuing with her education, she quickly crumbles after a visit from Maestra Oliviero. The sense of inferiority Elena's mother feels in the presence of the schoolteacher leads her to become completely acquiescent (although she is furious at being railroaded into the decision after she leaves). By the end of the novel, Lila has succeeded in rising above her origins in the only way left available to her – by marrying the richest young man in the neighborhood. While Elena envies the trappings of Lila's nouveau riche lifestyle, however, she dreams of rising above the neighborhood altogether through the twin goals of writing and marrying Nino. By virtue of her education, she feels she no longer belongs in her own social class but has not yet found the means of elevating herself to the next one.

Identity & Boundaries

In a novel that centres around Lila's erasure of herself from her own life, identity is a continual theme. Lila's decision to disappear and remove all traces of herself from her home intriguingly also reflects Ferrante's deliberate anonymity as an author.

In many ways, the identities of Elena and Lila consist of completely opposing characteristics. Elena is fair, Lila is dark, Elena seeks approval, Lila doesn't care what anyone thinks of her, when things go well for Elena things go badly for Lila, and vice versa.

While Lila's actions suggest that she has a strong sense of autonomy, Elena feels that she barely exists without Lila. When Elena is with Lila she thinks she feels her friend's energy flowing into her but, without her, she feels a sense of lack. The feeling that she lacks a clear sense of identity is exacerbated as she goes through adolescence and struggles to get used to the changes to her physical appearance – some days feeling attractive and on other occasions convinced that she is ugly. As Elena continually defines herself against Lila, her sense of self is further disrupted when Lila transforms, almost overnight, from an ugly duckling into a swan. No longer even able to console herself that she is the pretty one, Elena's self-esteem plummets.

Interestingly, although Lila appears to be the character with the strongest sense of identity, it is she who suffers from episodes of 'dissolving margins'. These episodes involve a strange sense that the boundaries between people and the rest of the world are dissolving. In the incident on New Year's Eve, she feels a sense of horror as the outlines of people at the party seem to be disappearing. In another incident, Lila describes her terror when a copper pot explodes while she is washing dishes. Significantly this episode takes place while Lila's family are pressuring her to marry Marcello Solara. For Lila, the distorted copper pot represents her fear that she will break altogether if she is forced into a shape that does not suit her. Lila's fear of dissolving margins or boundaries is also expressed in her reluctance to cross geographical boundaries. We learn from Elena at the beginning of the novel that Lila never leaves Naples, and her fear of venturing beyond the confines of the neighborhood is illustrated in the episode where, on her suggestion, she and Elena try to reach the sea. Lila's sudden decision to turn back indicates her fear of what lies beyond the neighborhood. It also suggests that she believes she can only really be herself within those geographical confines.

Surprisingly, despite Elena's seemingly fragile sense of identity, she is much more open to crossing geographical boundaries. While Lila fears leaving the confines of the neighborhood, Elena's fear is that she will never escape them. She first feels the boundaries of her world expanding when she is a teenager and her father takes her to Naples to show her the sights. Entranced by the view of the sea and Vesuvius, she feels that the world holds great possibilities. Similarly, when she first crosses the boundaries of the neighborhood with Lila, Elena is the one who wants to keep going until they reach the sea. As the novel progresses, Elena's boundaries expand as she gradually sees more of the world that lies outside the neighborhood. As she does so, she increasingly feels that her true identity lies not within the neighborhood but outside of it.

Language

In Elena's narrative she often refers to the way the other characters use language. The clear distinction she makes between those who speak Neapolitan dialect and those who speak Italian tells us a great deal about class, education and Elena's aspirations.

The majority of the characters who live in the neighborhood speak in Neapolitan dialect, which is very much a spoken rather than a written language. This reflects their poor and uneducated status, as proper Italian was a language reserved for the middle classes.

When she is a child, one of the things that impresses Elena

about Lila is that, while she frequently hurls obscene insults at her classmates in dialect, she is also able to converse in 'a beautiful, educated type of Italian' with the teachers. For Elena, this aptitude for language demonstrates Lila's great potential and singles her out as something special.

As the novel progresses Elena's preoccupation with language continues. Gradually acquiring an increasingly refined Italian vocabulary herself, she continues to be drawn to those who share this skill. Her obsession with Nino is partly due to the fact that he is also able to speak 'a literary Italian'. For Elena, a fine command of Italian represents the educated world that she aspires to enter into. At the end of the novel, Elena is struck for the first time by the rough language the boys of the neighborhood use. At that moment she realises, in order to still fit in with her old friends, she has to 'suppress' or 'diminish' herself by communicating with them in the same kind of language.

Books & Writing

In *My Brilliant Friend* books are presented as the key to knowledge and a better future. Elena and Lila bond as they read *Little Women* together and begin to share a dream that, if they study hard, they will be able to write similar books and raise themselves out of poverty. Shortly afterwards, Lila's dreams of continuing her formal education are dashed, while Elena's parents allow her to continue studying. When Elena follows Lila one day, however, she learns that her friend has been continuing her education in secret by borrowing books from the lending library. Lila's self-education from books means that she becomes proficient in the classics before her formally educated friend.

While Elena feels she has to compete with Lila in almost every arena, the area she cares most about is writing. When the two girls agree to write a book together and then Lila produces a story called 'The Blue Fairy' on her own, Elena is hurt but also struck by the brilliance of Lila's writing. After this point Lila gives up on the idea of becoming a writer while Elena, inspired by Donato Sarratore's published book of poems, feels that her sense of identity rests upon becoming a published author. Despite her determination to pursue her dream, however, Elena always feels as if Lila is the true writer. When she receives a letter from Lila while staying on Ischia,

56

Elena is immediately struck by the effortless, authentic quality of her friend's writing. Later, when the style of one of her school papers is highly praised by a teacher, Elena realises that she has been trying to adopt Lila's fluid writing style and has succeeded. As a result, Elena's writing successes always feel slightly fraudulent as they reflect as much of Lila's voice as her own. The amalgam of voices in Elena's writing style is particularly relevant when it comes to writing *My Brilliant Friend*. The idea that Elena has absorbed something of Lila's voice somehow makes it more appropriate that she should be the one to tell the story of Lila's life, as well as her own.

IMAGERY

The Copper Pot

When Don Achille is killed in his own home, Lila gruesomely describes her imagined vision of the murder scene. The intricate detail of her description includes blood spurting from Don Achille's neck and hitting 'a copper pot hanging on the wall'. Lila's focus on this detail is later echoed in her description (in a letter to Elena) of an incident which particularly frightens her. While she is washing dishes in the kitchen, a big copper pot explodes, 'as if it could no longer maintain its appearance as a pot.' This incident takes place during the period when Lila's parents are putting pressure on her to marry Marcello and makes her feel as if everything around her will break if she cannot find a solution to her predicament. The fear Lila experiences when she sees the unrecognisably distorted form of the copper pot reflects her fear that her own identity will be horribly distorted or irreparably broken if she is forced into a role that is repugnant to her.

Elena highlights the connection between the image of the broken pot and identity when she says that she always thinks of the copper pot whenever she notices 'a fracture in her or in me.' Elena has this feeling when she observes Lila and Stefano together, suggesting that she feels that her friend is, once again, being forced to take a shape that is unsuited to her. Nevertheless, her instinct

57

tells her that, 'no form could ever contain Lila, and that sooner or later she would break everything again.' The connection between Lila's identity and the broken pot is also echoed on the day of Lila's wedding when she bathes in a huge copper bath tub. As Lila washes, Elena is struck by 'the impression that the copper of the tub had a consistency not different from Lila's flesh, which was smooth, solid, calm.'

Shoes

Shoes take on an increasing significance for Lila as the novel progresses. When she is denied the opportunity to continue her education, Lila throws her energies into the only other outlet she is offered: her father's shoe shop. Through her beautiful shoe designs, she is able to express her creativity. They also provide the opportunity for a business project which has the potential to help her and her family escape poverty.

Lila's shoe designs also play a key role in her relationship with Stefano. When he buys the first pair of shoes that Lila and Rino made together and insists upon framing her designs, Stefano appears to appreciate how much of herself Lila has poured into the project. The importance Lila places on this appreciation is emphasised when, as evidence of Stefano's love for her, she tells Elena that her fiancé becomes sentimental whenever he handles the shoes. The almost magical symbolism that shoes take on in their relationship is reflected in Lila's decision to wear shoes she has designed herself on her wedding day.

The climax of the entire novel also revolves around shoes when Marcello Solara makes his entrance at the wedding reception. Marcello's presence indicates a double betrayal of Lila by Stefano. While he has broken his promise that Marcello will not attend the wedding, worse still, he has given him the first pair of shoes that Lila made. Stefano's casual betrayal of Lila's dreams suggests that business is ultimately more important to him than sentiment and bodes ill for their future marriage.

Fairy Tales

Throughout *My Brilliant Friend* Ferrante plays upon fairy tale imagery and its connotations. Lila writes a brilliant fairy tale when

58

she is a child called 'The Blue Fairy'. This is significant because her own life has several parallels with well-known fairy tales. Her instigation of the confrontation with Don Achille (who the girls imagine to be a hideous ogre with a big black bag) is reminiscent of 'Jack and the Beanstalk'. Meanwhile, as the daughter of a poor shoe repairer, her dreams of escaping poverty through her magical footwear designs have unmistakable overtones of 'The Elves and the Shoemaker'.

Lila's engagement draws upon more than one fairy tale romance. Elena enviously observes that Stefano kisses Lila 'the way princes kiss sleeping beauties'. At the same time, Lila undergoes a Cinderella-like transformation in appearance when she begins to wear the expensive clothes that Stefano buys for her. This leaves Elena feeling like a less glamorous character from a fairy tale by contrast (the Ugly Duckling). Not only does Stefano transform Lila's appearance and standard of living, he also dons the mantle of Fairy Godmother when he fulfils his future wife's wish, making it possible for her shoe designs to be turned into a reality.

Ferrante creates these romantic fairy tale images, only to tear them apart and reveal the prosaic truth that lies beneath them. Don Achille turns out to be an unattractive but otherwise ordinary looking man whose 'black bag' is a euphemism for his involvement with the black market. Similarly, when Elena leaves her broken spectacles with Lila, she imagines 'some miraculous intervention by Rino with his shoemaker's tools', only to discover that Stefano has paid an optician to mend them. Most significant of all in this debunking of fairy tale romance is the scene where Stefano tries on the shoes that Lila and her brother have made. In an almost comic reversal of the roles in Cinderella, Lila kneels in front of Stefano with a shoe horn, while he tries to squeeze his feet into her creations. The fact that the shoes are too tight (although Stefano insists on taking them anyway) should suggest to Lila that her future husband may be an ugly sister rather than the prince she has taken him for.

Dolls

The motif of dolls appears surprisingly frequently in Elena Ferrante's fiction. An earlier novel by Ferrante, *The Lost Daughter*, revolves around an incident where a middle-aged woman finds a young girl's doll on the beach and, for reasons of her own, chooses not to return it. Meanwhile, Ferrante's latest publication (a story for children) is told in the voice of Celina, the lost doll from her earlier novel.

In *My Brilliant Friend* dolls play a significant role in cementing the friendship between Elena and Lila. Before they become friends, Elena and Lila parallel-play with their dolls in the same courtyard while studiously ignoring each other. Significantly, the way the dolls look reflects the way their owners are perceived by others at this point. Elena is healthy-looking, fair and pretty, as is her doll, Tina. Lila's doll, Nu, however, is 'ugly and grimy', reflecting the scruffy, feral appearance of her mistress.

The moment the girls silently exchange their dolls marks a change in their relationship. When Lila drops Tina down the grate into the cellar below, Elena is devastated but is careful not to show it. Realising that she has already lost the doll, she somehow understands that any future friendship with Lila depends upon her reaction to the loss. After only a moment's hesitation, she responds by throwing Nu down the cellar after Tina. This incident sets the template for their future friendship. Wherever Lila leads, Elena promptly follows.

After failing to find the dolls in the cellar, Lila concludes that the fearsome Don Achille must have scooped them up in his black bag. This leads to the two girls confronting the 'ogre' who gives them the money to buy new dolls. Significantly, instead of dolls, the girls choose to buy a copy of *Little Women*. This choice demonstrates that the girls are outgrowing childish things and becoming 'little women' themselves. On another level, this incident also highlights their ambivalence towards traditional female roles. Playing with dolls is, of course, a way for girls to practise being mothers and, in Ferrante's other fiction, dolls are usually connected to conflicting emotions about motherhood. The fact that Lila and Elena choose a book over a doll suggests that, at this point, they believe that education is the key to the kind of future that they want. This is emphasised when both girls decide that they will make their fortune by becoming writers after reading the novel. For readers planning to read all four novels in the Neapolitan quartet, the link between the girls' dolls and motherhood is used again, to shocking effect, in *The Story of the Lost Child*.

Decay

When Enzo presents Lila with a garland of sorb apples Elena observes that, when they become overripe, the attractive fruits become brown, wrinkled and mushy, 'in a way that reminded me of the corpses of rats along the *stradone*'. This observation is echoed when Maestra Oliviero harshly points out that, while Lila's brilliance of mind has morphed into physical beauty, the effects are fleeting and, once she has passed her prime, Lila will be left with nothing. The connection Ferrante makes between overripe fruit and the ephemeral nature of youth is reminiscent of the Nature Morte works painted by the Dutch Masters. These paintings, which often depicted bowls of fruit just at the point of rotting, were intended to be an uncomfortable reminder to the viewer that, no matter how young, rich or beautiful they might be, death still awaited them. This cheery sentiment also bubbles under the surface of *My Brilliant Friend*. While Elena and Lila are at the point where they feel their lives are just beginning, Ferrante reminds the reader of how quickly life passes.

The images of decay in the novel also reflect the corruption that the very foundations of the neighborhood are built upon. The richest and most glamorous families in the neighborhood (the Solaras and the Carraccis) have made their money through a history of loan-sharking, smuggling, vote-rigging and other illegal activities, while the other neighborhood families are mired in poverty. Strongly affected by what she learns from Pasquale about the historical chain of corruption in the neighborhood, Lila becomes obsessed with the idea that corruption is in the blood of every one of them.

Vesuvius

The active volcano, Mount Vesuvius, can be glimpsed from the neighborhood and its lurking presence brilliantly symbolises the sense of potential explosion that rumbles through the novel. This mood is embodied in Lila, who continually gives the impression that, like the copper pot, or Vesuvius itself, she may unpredictably explode with violent rage at any moment. It is also reflected in the undercurrent of violence that seems to lurk everywhere and occasionally erupts into fights or domestic violence. Lila's luxurious apartment in the new neighborhood has a clear view of Vesuvius and readers are left to ponder its significance.

CHARACTERS

Ferrante provides an index of her characters at the beginning of the novel for good reason. Her large cast, which includes several generations of a number of different families, rivals that of a Dickens novel and can be confusing. In the later books in the Neapolitan quartet, almost all of these characters continue to have a role in the story.

Rafaella Cerullo (Lila)

My Brilliant Friend begins when Elena discovers that her sixty-six-year-old friend, Lila Cerullo, has disappeared without leaving a trace. Although arguably the most prominent character in the novel, we only get to know Lila (who is known to everyone else as Lina) through Elena's account of her. This means we are not party to her thought processes and actions but only Elena's interpretation of them. As a result, she is an enigmatic figure. The motivation behind her often unpredictable behaviour is worthy of endless speculation.

Right from the beginning of their relationship Lila represents everything Elena is not. While Elena is cautious, unthreateningly pretty and likes to be liked, Lila resembles a young Heathcliff in *Wuthering Heights*. Always dirty, with a feral manner, Lila couldn't care less that she is universally hated by the other children in the neighborhood and seems to enjoy conflict. Her aggressive manner is combined with a ruthless honesty that sometimes borders on malice. Lila's impulsive behaviour and tendency to invite danger into her life continues as she becomes a young woman. She represents the path the more circumspect of us fear we might find ourselves on if we allowed our impulses free reign.

Even as a child, however, Lila's less attractive qualities are to some degree countered by positive character traits. She adores her

63

brother, Rino, and worries constantly about his welfare. While often riding roughshod over Elena's feelings, she is also fiercely protective of her friend, as illustrated in the scene where she threatens Marcello Solara with a knife when he touches Elena. Lila also shows great empathy towards the suffering of Melina, whose mental instability is treated as something of a joke by the rest of the neighborhood.

Lila's intuitive understanding of Melina's suffering demonstrates her ability to see things that others don't. It is this intense sensitivity to the world around her that leads Lila to feel as if people and objects are always on the verge of breaking their boundaries. Her episodes of 'dissolving margins', and her disproportionate fear when she sees a copper pot explode, reflect her anxiety that the boundaries of her own identity will strain and break. It is this fear of dissolving boundaries which seems to lie behind Lila's reluctance to stray beyond the boundaries of the neighborhood.

One of the strongest driving forces behind Lila's personality is her fierce intelligence. A brilliant student in all subjects, she writes a story, at the age of ten, in which Elena enviously spots creative genius. When her father refuses her request to continue her education beyond elementary school and her teacher, Maestra Oliviero, consequently withdraws her support, Lila's intellectual gifts become a curse. With only the outlets of housework or shoemaking available to her, she opts for the latter, pouring her creativity and intelligence into extraordinary shoe designs and a plan to expand the business. In place of her studies, she intellectually engages with politics as she begins to connect her personal experiences with what is going on in the wider world.

Elena is attracted by Lila's intelligence and by the impression she gives of living life more intensely than anyone else. Enchanted by the energy of Lila's speech and her gestures, Elena feels that their magic rubs off on her is some way. It is this intense energy, combined with Lila's blossoming beauty, which also has an electrifying effect upon the boys of the neighborhood. Elena observes when they go dancing together that, although there are more curvaceous girls in the room, all the boys' eyes are on Lila: 'something had begun to emanate from Lila's mobile body that the males sensed, an energy that dazed them.' Lila's sexual magnetism soon provokes violent outbursts among jealous men wherever she goes. This is illustrated at the party where personal and political rivalries between Pasquale, Stefano, Antonio and the Solara brothers all come to a head as the young men compete to dance with Lila.

While Lila's sexual attractiveness gives her power over men, she also becomes a victim of it. Trapped in a situation where she can ensure her family's future, but only by marrying a man she detests, she takes the only other available option by accepting the advances of an equally wealthy man. Interestingly, Lila shows little interest in sex herself, revealing to a shocked Elena that she has done nothing more than kiss Stefano. She also expresses disgust at the idea of performing oral sex with any man. This suggests that the raw sexuality that the male characters believe Lila exudes is, in reality, an entirely different kind of energy or power.

Of all the characters in the novel, Lila comes the closest to being a feminist. As a child, she competes against and generally beats the boys in every arena. Later, while all the other teenage girls are swooning over the Solara brothers, Lila despises them for their lack of respect towards women. Lila also comes to represent the simmering anger of the women of the neighborhood in general. Her certainty that the murderer of Don Achille was a woman demonstrates her comprehension that women's desires and ambitions are thwarted by a dearth of opportunity. Sadly, by the end of the novel, although Lila has attempted to take control of her destiny as best as she can, her horizons will be limited within the confines of marriage. Her insistence that Elena must continue studying and be her 'brilliant friend' is an acknowledgment that this path is irrevocably closed to her. In Lila's fate, Ferrante mourns the waste of female intelligence.

Fernando Cerullo

Lila's father owns a small shoe repair business. His traditional attitudes are demonstrated in his refusal to let his daughter study beyond elementary school and his reluctance to modernise his business.

Fernando's behaviour is symptomatic of the ingrained patriarchal structure of the family in the neighborhood. While Elena observes that, when unprovoked, he is 'a kind, sympathetic man', she also witnesses him hurl Lila out of a window during an

65

argument. Fernando makes it clear to Lila that the future of her whole family lies in her answer to Marcello's proposal. When Lila says that she would rather drown herself than marry Marcello, he threatens to break every bone in her body.

Nunzia Cerullo

Lila's mother is a background figure whose lack of presence reflects her lack of power within the Cerullo household. When Maestra Oliviero wants to persuade Lila's parents to allow their daughter to continue her education, she asks Nunzia to come into school to see examples of Lila's brilliant work. While Nunzia complies, she continues to refuse consent as she cannot overrule her husband.

Rino Cerullo

Lila's brother, Rino, is six years older than his sister. Unlike Lila, he is not academically gifted and begins to learn the craft of repairing shoes in his father's shop from the age of ten.

Rino shares Lila's aggressive and reckless temperament but lacks the intelligence to constructively channel these traits. Although he is supposed to act as Lila's chaperone when she ventures out of the neighborhood, he becomes an increasing liability, often initiating ugly confrontations which his younger sister frequently has to rescue him from.

The pent-up rage exhibited by Rino stems from his sense of powerlessness. While he dreams of escaping poverty and becoming rich, he is aware that, in all likelihood, he will follow in the footsteps of his father and remain a poor shoe repairer. Rino's dreams of wealth are reflected in his unhealthy obsession with the Solara brothers, whom he envies and dislikes, and his ambition to expand his father's business into handmade shoemaking. Desperate to prevent her brother from becoming involved in organised crime, Lila turns his business ambitions into a reality with the help of Stefano's money.

While Rino is a continual burden to Lila, he shows genuine affection for his sister when he tries to persuade their father to let her go to middle school, even offering to pay for her if his father pays for his help in the shoe shop.

Gennaro (Rino)

Lila's son, Rino, is named after Lila's brother. At the beginning of the novel he contacts Elena to tell her about his mother's disappearance. Elena has little time for Rino, who has clearly not inherited his mother's drive and determination. Although forty years old, Elena reflects that he has never worked and is 'a small time crook and spendthrift.'

Elena Greco

Elena (also known as Lenuccia or Lenu) is the narrator of *My Brilliant Friend*. Her coming-of-age story is written with hindsight as she begins it at the age of sixty-six when her lifelong friend, Lila, disappears. Her narration is also far from objective. Angry at her friend for 'overdoing it as usual', the act of writing their story becomes an act of revenge through which she refuses to allow her friend to erase herself ('We'll see who wins this time, I said to myself.') Elena is also emotionally invested in the events she describes.

Interestingly, although Elena has younger siblings (Peppe, Gianni and Elisa) she barely mentions them in her narrative. Instead, her childhood world revolves almost entirely around her friend, Lila. Elena's fixation with Lila seems to spring from the fact that, at least on the surface, the girls are the complete antithesis of each other. Elena is fair, Lila is dark; Elena is needy and craves approval, Lila is autonomous and hostile; Elena is cautious and often feels emotionally detached from life, while Lila is hypersensitive to the world around her and impulsively acts on her desires. For Elena, Lila subconsciously represents the dark side of herself which she both fears and longs to set free.

Elena's obsession with Lila is so intense that she begins to define herself almost entirely through her friend. While Lila sets the benchmark of achievement (in school, in writing style and, later, in attractiveness to the opposite sex), Elena continually struggles to keep up. Lila's influence encourages Elena to push herself and achieve academic success (a motivation she seems to lack if left to her own devices). On the other hand, it has an extremely unhealthy impact on her self-esteem. As the two girls are complete opposites in both looks and personality, Elena comes to feel that only Lila's qualities are of value. Although she realises that it isn't good for her to spend her time 'feeling diminished', Elena finds herself unable to cut Lila out of her life. Without Lila she feels her life becomes dull and purposeless.

While Lila is the most powerful influence on Elena, Ferrante makes it clear that Elena's mother also has an impact on her sense of identity. Elena is shockingly honest when recounting the feelings of revulsion her mother's limp and wayward right eye inspire in her. Elena's preoccupation with these physical imperfections reflects her realisation that her mother was once a vibrant and attractive young woman. Although Elena is reluctant to ask her mother about the cause of her leg injury, she associates it with the life of poverty and domestic drudgery that she has led – a life Elena does not want to replicate in any way. Significantly, when Elena goes through a period of psychological crisis, she dreams that her mother is emerging from her body and, afterwards, becomes anxious at the thought that she will wake up one morning to find that her legs no longer work properly. This anxiety demonstrates Elena's desire to escape the life of her mother and the fear that she will not.

Despite Elena's many insecurities, she is the one who goes on to further study with increasing success, becoming the 'brilliant friend' she has always considered Lila to be. Even then, however, Elena's academic successes are always marred by the nagging belief that it is Lila who possesses the real intellect. A number of the pieces of work Elena's teachers praise her for are influenced either by Lila's ideas or writing style. While Elena has much to be proud of, she feels that her own achievements are a pale imitation of what her friend could achieve given the opportunity. Readers are left to decide for themselves whether Elena would have been perceived as such a gifted student without the equally malign and inspiring influence of Lila.

By the end of the novel, Elena's studies have led her into a social no man's land. While she doesn't yet possess the confidence to feel comfortable in the world of the educated middle-classes, represented by Professor Galiani, Elena realises that she has to 'suppress' or 'diminish' herself in order to mix with her old friends from the neighborhood. Feeling completely isolated at Lila's wedding reception, she makes a significant decision when she pulls away from the grip of both her mother and Antonio to go and sit with the more intellectual Nino Sarratore. This decision demonstrates that she has chosen a life of the intellect which she hopes will help her to escape the neighborhood. While this seems to be a gesture of independence on Elena's part, Ferrante also makes us aware that it is Elena's heart as well as her head that influences this decision. Hopelessly in love with Nino, she sees his guidance, rather than her own intelligence, as the key to her future.

Signora Greco

Elena's portrait of her mother is not a flattering one. As well as criticising her physical flaws, Elena suggests that her mother is cold and unloving towards her. Ferrante undercuts Elena's unsympathetic commentary, however, by including a number of incidents that suggest her daughter does not do her justice. While she is not a demonstrative parent, Elena's mother demonstrates her love through small actions. The incident where she allows her daughter to wear her treasured silver bracelet as a reward for her success in school speaks of a pride in Elena's academic achievements. Meanwhile, the episode where Signora Greco turns up at Maestra Oliviero's with an umbrella for Elena (only to discover her daughter has lied about her whereabouts) demonstrates a protective maternal instinct which Elena doesn't believe her mother possesses.

With a typically teenage lack of sympathy, Elena thinks of her mother as everything she doesn't want to become. When Elena describes hearing her mother 'angrily crushing with her heel the cockroaches that came through the front door', Ferrante also makes it clear that a life of poverty and domestic servitude is not one that Signora Greco would have willingly chosen either.

Signor Greco

Elena's father is a porter at the City Hall. Less conventional than Lila's father, he allows his daughter to continue with her education and takes some pride in her achievements. Signor Greco plays an important part in expanding Elena's horizons when he spends a day showing his daughter the sights of Naples. Elena sees a new side to her father, who seems more relaxed outside the neighborhood. The outing also makes her realise that there is a much wider world waiting for her if she can escape the confines of the neighborhood.

Don Achille Carracci

Described in the index of characters as 'the ogre of fairy tales', Don Achille is a notorious loan shark and a dealer in the black market. When they are children, Elena and Lila are aware that the entire neighborhood fears and hates Don Achille but they don't know why. As a consequence, Elena imagines him as a creature something like the Gruffalo, 'covered with purple boils' and carrying an enormous black bag.

When Don Achille is murdered, the Solaras, who are also involved in organised crime, become the most feared family in the neighborhood.

Maria Carracci

Don Achille's wife continues to work in the family grocery store after the death of her husband.

Stefano Carracci

The elder son of Don Achille, Stefano is several years older than Elena and Lila. Although he is uneducated and speaks 'almost exclusively in dialect', he has a good head for business and expands the family grocery store into a thriving concern.

Stefano's courtship of Lila begins when he invites the girls to celebrate New Year at his house. When the girls explain that they already have plans with their friends, Stefano extends the invitation to the entire neighborhood, including the family of the man who allegedly murdered his father. While Lila views this extended invitation as a noble gesture of forgiveness and an indication that he wants to draw a line under past family feuds, it is clear that Stefano's one motivation is to be close to Lila. Lila's naivety concerning Stefano's motivations continues into their relationship. Lila increasingly sees Stefano in the role of a saviour, as he helps her escape a marriage to Marcello Solara, while also helping her family to expand their business. Lila believes that Stefano's actions are motivated by love for her, and his emotional reaction when he holds the first pair of shoes that she designed seems to support her belief. When Marcello Solara walks into their wedding reception wearing that very same pair of shoes, however, Stefano's integrity is seriously brought into question. Not only has he broken his promise to Lila that the Solara brothers will not be at the wedding, he also demonstrates, by selling the shoes to Marcello, that he prioritises money over love.

Alfonso Carracci

Don Achille's younger son, Alfonso, is one of the brightest boys in Elena's elementary class. While the other children avoid competing with Alfonso, due to his family's fearsome reputation, Lila beats him in a maths competition, leading him to go home in tears. The repercussions of the incident ripple through the neighborhood as Alfonso's older brother, Stefano, threatens to prick Lila's tongue with a pin, Lila's brother, Rino, starts a fight with Stefano, and Don Achille's wife, Maria, insults Lila's mother. To bring hostilities to a close, Lila's father publicly apologises to Don Achille. The episode illustrates not only the power of the Carracci family in the neighborhood but also Lila's unwillingness to conform to the unwritten rules about not upsetting them.

Like Elena, Alfonso continues his studies and they become good friends. Well-mannered, sensitive and handsome, Alfonso becomes the boyfriend of Marisa Sarratore at the end of the novel.

Pinuccia Carracci

Don Achille's daughter has a small role in *My Brilliant Friend* but becomes a more important character in the later Neapolitan novels. She becomes romantically involved with Rino, Lila's brother, at the end of the novel.

Alfredo Peluso

Alfredo Peluso is the neighborhood carpenter and is known to be a communist. Criticised by his neighbours for failing to adequately support his family, he attributes his financial ruin to Don Achille and gambles away any money he has in the Bar Solara. When Don

71

Achille is murdered, Alfredo is convicted of the crime and sent to prison, leaving his family on the point of destitution. When he is arrested, Alfredo proclaims his innocence and it is never made clear whether his arrest is based on solid evidence, or whether it has more to do with his unpopular political beliefs.

Giuseppina Peluso

The wife of Alfredo.

Pasquale Peluso

The eldest son of Alfredo, Pasquale is a construction worker and a militant communist. He is the first of the boys to declare his love for Lila, causing Elena great disappointment as she, at first, thinks he is interested in her. By the end of the novel he has paired up with Ada Cappuccio.

Pasquale is the first of Elena's peer group to display strong political convictions. While Elena and most of her friends remain largely ignorant of current affairs and politics, Pasquale points out the historical chain of corruption that lies behind the social hierarchy of the neighborhood. His claim that Don Achille was a spy for the Nazi Fascists inspires an awakening political consciousness in Lila (although this does not prevent her marrying Don Achille's son).

While Pasquale's political convictions are entirely genuine, they become inextricably tangled with his unrequited love for Lila. His attacks upon the Solara brothers and Stefano are motivated just as much by sexual jealousy as political righteousness.

Carmela Peluso (Carmen)

When Lila realises that Elena is to take the admissions test for middle school and she cannot, she begins to spend her time with Pasquale's sister, Carmela. Like Lila, Carmela is also fated not to go to middle school and, instead, becomes a sales clerk in a dry goods store. With Elena in tow, the three girls become 'a trio' in which Elena jealously reflects she always feels 'the third'. Like Elena, Carmela is in awe of Lila and tries to imitate her walk and speech patterns. In Carmela, Elena sees her own behaviour unwelcomely reflected back at her.

When Carmela confides that she is in love with Alfonso Carracci, Elena is deeply struck by the romantic notion of the daughter of a murderer falling in love with the son of the victim. As it turns out, however, it is Lila who has planted the idea in Carmela's impressionable mind. By the end of the novel she seems to have got over her romantic crush and has paired up with Enzo.

Melina Cappuccio

Melina lives in the same apartment building as Elena's family. Although only in her early thirties, she is a widow and has six children. Perhaps unsurprisingly, she is also mentally unstable. After the death of her husband, Melina receives help from Donato Sarratore who lives in the apartment above. When their relationship turns into an affair, Melina begins to persecute Donato's wife, Lidia. One day Elena sees the two women rolling down the stairs as they fight. Shortly afterwards, the Sarratore family leave the neighborhood, sending Melina into a further mental decline.

Melina is a distant relative of Lila's mother and, while the other children tend to ridicule her, Lila is 'deeply affected' by the mad widow. This is illustrated when Lila violently slaps Marisa for hurling insults at Melina, who is eating soap out of a paper bag. Lila's preoccupation with Melina's decline into madness demonstrates that she not only sympathises with Melina but also identifies with her. Showing a wisdom beyond her years, Lila understands how a woman in Melina's position could easily descend into madness. She also seems to fear that the same fate may await her.

Ada Cappuccio

Melina's daughter, Ada, is fourteen years old when the Solara brothers publicly pull her into their car and then bring her back an hour later. While she doesn't seem upset by the incident, the fact that the Solara brothers feel able to treat her in this disrespectful way emphasises that, as a poor and fatherless girl with a mad mother, Ada falls at the very bottom of the social scale. By the end of the novel she pairs up with Pasquale.

73

Antonio Cappuccio

Melina's son, Antonio, is a mechanic and bears the burden of both the death of his father and the mental instability of his mother. He also feels forced to defend his sister's honour when she is picked up by the Solara brothers and, as a result, is beaten 'bloody' by them.

When Antonio asks Elena if she will be his girlfriend she agrees, even though she has no romantic feelings towards him. Her decision is mainly prompted by the desire to keep up with Lila by having a boyfriend. Antonio is grateful and devoted but becomes a casualty of Elena's unrequited passion for Nino. After getting into debt by buying a new suit to accompany Elena to Lila's wedding, he finds himself ignored by his date as soon as Nino arrives.

Donato Sarratore

Donato Sarratore appears to be a pillar of the community. A serious man with a wife and five children, he works for the state railway and regularly attends church. Donato is considered 'womanish' by the other men of the neighborhood as he appears to be devoted to his family, does the grocery shopping and even looks after the baby. He is also a great womaniser, however, and the apparently charitable assistance that he offers Melina is a prelude to seduction. Despite Melina's mental fragility, Donato thinks nothing of hurting her and the fallout of the affair leads to his entire family having to move out of the neighborhood.

Although it is clear to the reader from early on what kind of a man Donato is, Elena initially views him through rose-tinted glasses, influenced by the knowledge that he has published a book. The publication of his small volume of poetry strikes the naïve Elena as an extraordinary achievement for someone from the neighborhood and she views Donato as an inspirational figure. As a result, she comes to see his relationship with Melina as a tragic love affair. When she spends time with the Sarratore family in Ischia, Elena is still inclined to think well of him, noting his chivalrous manners and the ease with which he compliments all the women. She is surprised to observe, however, that the published author shows no interest in literature, only ever reading aloud an article which he turns out to have written himself. Elena's rude awakening to Donato's true character comes when he sexually molests her, leaving her disgusted and ashamed.

Lidia Sarratore

Despite her husband's constant philandering, Donato's wife, Lidia, appears surprisingly content in her marriage. It is unclear whether she is in denial over Donato's serial adultery or if she simply chooses to live with it.

Nino Sarratore

Nino, the eldest of the Sarratores' five children, is the object of Elena's unrequited passions. She is attracted not only by his 'rebellious hair' and 'intense eyes' but also by what he seems to represent to her. Nino's knowledgeable air and ability to speak 'a literary Italian' are characteristics which Elena covets and sees as her key to escaping the neighborhood. Interestingly, Nino also has some common characteristics with Elena's other great love, Lila. Both are forceful in their opinions and uninterested in the approval of others. Most significantly of all, they both give off an aura of restless dissatisfaction. As Elena observes, 'Nino has something that's eating him inside, like Lila, and it's a gift and a suffering'.

Elena seems to get off to a promising start with Nino when he pushes her against a wall and tells her that he wants her to become engaged to him. Flustered, Elena fails to grasp the opportunity and, after this incident, Nino barely speaks to her, causing Elena to wonder if he even remembers her when she sees him again at high school. When they meet again on Ischia, Nino shows little interest in Elena, despite her puppy-like devotion.

Through Elena's responses to Nino, Ferrante brilliantly evokes the blinding effects of love. Elena chooses not to see the irony in Nino's assertion that he is nothing like his father, despite the fact that he clearly shares Donato's egotism and intellectual arrogance. She also chooses not to listen to the warning bells that must be ringing in her ears when Nino makes the strange admission that he always envied the friendship of Elena and Lila and imagined that, if he and Elena became engaged, all three of them would be together forever. There are also hints that Nino is not quite as intelligent as he thinks he is – expressed in Elena's surprise that Enzo and Alfonso both outshine Nino in the maths competitions at school and in Nino's jealousy when he realises that Elena is a better writer than him.

Elena's choice of Nino over Antonio, at the end of the novel, is a troubling one. While she and Nino are undoubtedly more intellectually suited, Nino has shown her none of the affection or devotion demonstrated by Antonio.

Marisa Sarratore

Marisa is the eldest daughter of Donato and Lidia and, unlike Nino, adores her father. Marisa is critical of her brother, telling Elena that he is 'cold-blooded' and 'closed up in himself'.

Pino, Clelia and Ciro Sarratore

The younger children of Donato and Lidia.

Nicola Scanno

The neighborhood fruit and vegetable seller.

Assunta Scanno

Nicola's wife.

Enzo Scanno

The son of Nicola and Assunta, Enzo is considered 'a dangerous child' at Elena's elementary school. At least three years older than the girls, he repeats a year but shows an unexpected gift for mathematics.

Angry after Lila beats him in a maths competition at school, Enzo leads a group of boys in throwing rocks at her. Lila retaliates with a sharp rock that makes Enzo's leg gush with blood and Enzo responds with a rock that hits Lila on the head, knocking her to the sidewalk. After the rock throwing incident, Enzo demonstrates his respect for Lila by presenting her with a garland of sorb apples. Later, he shows his continuing devotion to her by striding in to challenge Marcello Solara when he refuses to let go of Lila's arm after dancing with her. His role as Lila's protector continues into the later Neapolitan novels.

Despite his talent for mental arithmetic, Enzo is lazy at school and his teacher doesn't put him forward for the admission tests for middle school. Already working with his father, Enzo takes over his parents' fruit and vegetable business, travelling the neighborhood in a horse-drawn cart. He gains a reputation in the neighborhood for being hard-working and level-headed and pairs up with Carmen at the end of the novel.

Silvio Solara

The owner of the bar-pastry shop, Silvio is also involved in the Camorra (the Neapolitan version of the Mafia). Bar Solara is the favoured hangout for those involved in organised crime and, when Don Achille is murdered, Silvio becomes the new Godfather of the neighborhood.

Manuela Solara

Silvio's wife, Manuela, is a moneylender. Her red book of debtors is much feared in the neighborhood.

The Solara Brothers

The sons of Silvio Solara revel in their father's ill-gotten wealth and power, cruising the impoverished neighborhood in their Fiat 1100. While most of the girls of the neighborhood admire them, Lila detests the way the brothers arrogantly wield their power and threatens Marcello with a knife when he casually touches Elena's arm. Rather than holding a grudge against Lila, however, Marcello falls hopelessly in love with her. Despite hostile discouragement from her, he follows Lila around like a lost sheep and becomes determined to make her his wife.

Michele is the driving force behind the brothers. More intelligent than Marcello, he also possesses a more frightening capacity for violence, illustrated when Elena sees him wielding an iron bar in a fight with a 'cold ferocity'.

77

Signor Spagnuolo

The pastry maker at the Solara family's bar-pastry shop.

Rosa Spagnuolo

The wife of the pastry maker.

Gigliola Spagnuolo

Gigliola is in Elena's year at elementary school and continues with her to middle school. Instead of going on to high school, however, she goes to work with her parents in the pastry shop and becomes Michele Solara's girlfriend.

Gino

Gino, the son of the pharmacist, is the first member of the opposite sex to see Elena's breasts when he bets twenty lire that they are real. He later becomes Elena's first boyfriend. Elena brings their short-lived relationship to an end when Gino humiliates Alfonso by laughing at him in class.

Maestro Ferraro

Maestro Ferraro is a teacher who also runs the lending library at the elementary school. In recognition of their love of reading, he awards Lila and Elena prizes for the impressive number of books they borrow.

Maestra Oliviero

Maestra Oliviero is the competitive female teacher at Elena's elementary school. A strong woman with a feminist mindset, she is keen to prove herself better than her male colleagues by showing off her most brilliant students in mental arithmetic competitions.

Maestra Oliviero is the first to notice the academic potential of Elena and Lila and encourages them to educate their way to independence. While she successfully bullies Elena's parents into allowing her to stay on at school, however, she has less success with Lila's parents.

While Maestra Oliviero turns out to be a crucial mentor for Elena, her abandonment of Lila borders on cruelty. Once Maestra Oliviero accepts that Lila will not go on to middle school, her keen encouragement turns to cold disinterest. When Elena shows Maestra Oliviero the story Lila writes as a ten-year-old, rather than admitting its brilliance, she refers to the Cerullo family as 'plebs' and advises Elena to forget Lila and think of herself. Several years later, when Lila delivers a wedding invitation to her old teacher, Maestra Oliviero claims not to recognise her former pupil and shuts the door in her face. Lila is deeply hurt by Maestra Oliviero's unnecessarily harsh treatment of her. Ferrante suggests, however, that the teacher's actions spring from bitter disappointment at the waste of Lila's intelligence. Her claim not to recognise the expensively dressed young woman on the verge of marriage indicates that she can no longer see a trace of the young girl she once taught, who was brimming with potential.

Professor Gerace

Professor Gerace is the high school teacher who singles Elena out as a gifted student in Greek.

Professor Galiani

When Elena clashes with her religious education teacher about the nature of the Holy Spirit, Professor Galiani takes Elena's side. Elena is fascinated by the female professor as she is known to be a communist. She also embodies the possibilities open to highly educated women. In the later Neapolitan novels she becomes a significant guiding figure in Elena's life.

Nella Incardo

At Maestra Oliviero's suggestion, Elena goes to stay with the teacher's cousin, Nella, who runs a guesthouse in Barano on Ischia. The excursion is the first trip Elena makes away from home and she finds Nella, who is lively, liberated and independent, a refreshing change from her mother. Although it is never made explicit, there is more than a suggestion that Nella may be one of

79

Donato Sarratore's lovers. Her copy of the book of poetry written by Donato is dedicated to 'darling Nella' and she tells Elena that she has learned the poems by heart.

DISCUSSION QUESTIONS

1/ Discuss the opposing characteristics of Elena and Lila. Which character did you most sympathise with? What do they gain from each other?

2/ The moment when Lila drops Elena's doll into the cellar is crucial in the development of their friendship. How does this moment sum up the future dynamics of their relationship? Do you think the girls' treatment of their dolls has any other significance?

3/ Discuss Ferrante's unsentimental portrait of female friendship. How does it differ from other novels about friendship that you have read? Is the friendship Elena and Lila share normal or dysfunctional?

4/ How does Elena feel in Lila's absence? Why does she feel like this? Does Elena need Lila as much as she thinks she does?

5/ In the fourth Neapolitan novel, *The Story of the Lost Child*, Elena explains: 'I want to seek on the page a balance between her and me that in life I couldn't find even between myself and me.' Do you think her narrative equally balances her own life and Lila's? How does she capture Lila's experience without being able to describe her thought processes? Would you have liked to hear the story from Lila's perspective?

6/ Elena often chooses unflattering words to describe Lila ('dangerous', 'vicious', 'malicious' and even 'evil'). Do you think these terms are justified? Does Elena want the reader to dislike Lila?

7/ The incident where Elena and Lila unsuccessfully attempt to walk to the sea highlights surprising character traits in both girls.

What does it tell us about Elena and Lila? Do you think Elena might be right in suspecting ulterior motives for the escapade on Lila's part?

8/ Ferrante portrays Naples as a simmering cauldron of violence. What are the catalysts for this violence? How does it affect Elena, Lila and the other young people of the neighborhood?

9/ Discuss Elena's feelings about her mother. Do you think Elena is fair in her assessment of her mother? Why is she so fixated by her physical flaws?

10/ When Marcello Solara accidentally breaks Elena's bracelet and touches her wrist, Lila threatens him with a knife. Why does she react so violently? What is it about the Solara brothers that she despises so much?

11/ Why do you think Elena is attracted to Nino? Is he worthy of her affection?

12/ When Lila hits puberty she becomes a magnet for the young men of the neighborhood. Other than her beauty, what is it about her that attracts them? How do you think Lila feels about her sexual power?

13/ Elena describes Lila's transformation from an ugly duckling to a swan. Did you notice any other fairy tale imagery in the novel? Why do you think Ferrante draws on these images in what is essentially a realist novel?

14/ The normally fearless Lila is uncharacteristically frightened by witnessing a copper pot exploding and an incident on New Year's Eve when she feels the margins of the world are 'dissolving'. How are these two episodes linked? Why do they inspire such terror in Lila?

15/ Could you understand Lila's decision to marry Stefano rather than Marcello? Does she choose the right man? Are any other options open to her?

16/ What is the role of the elementary school teacher, Maestra Oliviero, in the novel? Why does she claim not to recognise Lila when she personally delivers an invitation to her wedding?

17/ In her narrative Elena makes a clear distinction between those who speak in Neapolitan dialect and those who speak Italian. What is the significance of this distinction? How does it reflect Elena's own aspirations?

18/ Were you surprised when Elena turned out to be the 'brilliant friend' in the friendship? Do you think the title refers to Elena or Lila?

19/ The climax of the novel comes when Marcello walks into Lila's wedding reception wearing the first pair of shoes she designed and helped to make. What is the significance of this seemingly minor incident? Why is Lila so upset? What does the incident indicate about Stefano's character?

20/ Does Ferrante offer any clues as to what the future holds for Elena and Lila? What do you think will happen to them?

21/ What is the meaning of Lila's disappearance at the beginning of the novel? Why does she cut herself out of the photographs in her home?

22/ Do you think Elena's decision to tell Lila's story is an act of love or revenge? Is her account entirely reliable?

23/ *My Brilliant Friend* boasts an enormous cast of characters which would put Charles Dickens to shame. Why do you think Ferrante includes so many characters in her novel? Are they all necessary? Did you find them difficult to keep track of?

24/ Elena Ferrante has deliberately avoided releasing information about herself, believing that her novels should stand on their own merit. Does the absence of information about the author detract from or enhance the novels? As the publishing world becomes more and more publicity driven, can you understand why Ferrante would choose to withhold her identity?

25/ Ferrante's authorial anonymity and her decision to call her narrator Elena has led readers to speculate that much of her subject matter is autobiographical. Would you agree? Does it matter?

26/ In her review of Ferrante's second Neapolitan novel, *The Story of a New Name*, Joan Frank writes: 'The through-line in all of Ferrante's investigations, for me, is nothing less than one long, mind-and-heart-shredding howl for the history of women'. Discuss this idea in relation to *My Brilliant Friend*.

27/ Some readers have suggested that only women can fully appreciate Elena Ferrante's novels. Do you think this is true or does she transcend the limitations of gender? Is there any possibility that the author of *My Brilliant Friend* could be a man?

28/ Fans of Ferrante have compared the addictive quality of the Neapolitan quartet to a literary soap opera. Has reading *My Brilliant Friend* inspired you to read the other Neapolitan novels?

QUIZ QUESTIONS

1/ How does Elena learn of Lila's disappearance?

2/ What are the names of the dolls belonging to Elena and Lila?

3/ What does Elena believe Don Achille carries around with him?

4/ Which novel do Elena and Lila read together and admire?

5/ Why does Stefano threaten to prick Lila's tongue with a pin?

6/ What is the title of the story that Lila writes as a girl?

7/ How does Lila break her arm?

8/ Which physical trait of her mother's is Elena particularly horrified by?

9/ Who does Lila believe murdered Don Achille?

10/ What do the girls see Melina eating out of a paper bag?

11/ Why does Elena initially admire Donato Sarratore?

12/ What does Elena's mother allow her daughter to wear as a reward for her academic achievements?

13/ Who does Lila threaten with a shoemaker's knife?

14/ What makes Lila think that Stefano wants to bring an end to the history of feuding in the neighborhood?

15/ Lila becomes extremely distressed when a household object unexpectedly breaks. What is it?

QUIZ ANSWERS

1/She receives a phone call from Lila's son, Rino

2/ Tina and Nu

3/ A big black bag

4/ *Little Women*

5/ Lila beats his younger brother, Alfonso, in a mathematics competition

6/ 'The Blue Fairy'

7/ Her father throws her out of the apartment window

8/ Her limp

9/ A woman

10/ Soap

11/ He has had a volume of poems published

12/ Her silver bracelet

13/ Marcello Solara

14/ He invites the entire neighborhood (including the family of the man accused of killing of his father) to his New Year's Eve party

15/ A copper pot

FURTHER READING

'The Neapolitan Quartet' by Elena Ferrante

Readers who loved *My Brilliant Friend* will need little urging to read the other three books in the Neapolitan quartet; *The Story of a New Name*, *Those Who Leave and Those Who Stay*, and *The Story of the Lost Child*.

The four novels together form a satisfying and addictive whole, taking Elena and Lila from young womanhood to old age. Although the lives of Elena and Lila take very different directions, the two women remain bound together by their intense bond. The novels also continue to follow the fates of other characters from *My Brilliant Friend*, whose lives intertwine with Elena and Lila in surprising ways. As well as building on the foundations of the plot in *My Brilliant Friend*, Ferrante embellishes on the themes and imagery introduced in the first novel.

The Woman Upstairs by Claire Messud

Nora, the narrator of this story, declares at the beginning of the novel that readers really do not want to know how angry she is. Of course we do and her flashback narrative examines not only the depth of her anger, but also its cause. At forty-two years old, Nora is single and childless. For these reasons she is all but invisible to the rest of society. Her life seems to take a turn for the better when she meets Sirena, a beautiful Italian artist who offers Nora an outlet for her frustrated artistic ambitions. Nora falls in love with Sirena's entire family and begins to believe that they are the key to her future. Her dreams are shattered, however, when she discovers an unforgivable betrayal which leads to her current state of fury.

Although quite different to *My Brilliant Friend* in subject matter, Messud's compelling novel explores similar themes: the restrictive nature of gender expectations and frustrated female creativity. Most importantly, like Ferrante's writing, it crackles with the energy of a woman's fury.

The Little Friend by Donna Tartt

Tartt's novel, first published in 2002, centres on twelve-year-old Harriet Cleve Dufesnes. Living in Mississippi in the early 1970s, Harriet is obsessed with getting to the bottom of the death of her nine-year-old brother Robin, who died under mysterious circumstances several years earlier. During a scorching summer she begins to trail Danny Ratcliff, a former classmate of Robin's, who has become a petty criminal. Convinced that Danny killed her brother, Harriet watches and waits for the right moment to take her revenge.

Like *My Brilliant Friend*, this is a very dark coming-of-age story. Tartt's portrayal of growing up within a fractured family in the violent atmosphere of the Deep South is utterly unsentimental. The fiercely intelligent Harriet also bears some similarities to Lila.

My Struggle by Karl Ove Knausgaard

Between 2009 and 2011 the Norwegian writer, Karl Ove Knausgaard, published six autobiographical novels under the series title *My Struggle*. One of the greatest Norwegian publishing successes ever, the books were translated into numerous languages. Although marketed as fiction, the books are clearly autobiographical while employing the techniques of fiction. Knausgaard writes about his life, from childhood onwards, with a brutal honesty and intensity that is often painful to read. Declared a masterpiece by many critics, *My Struggle* has also provoked controversy. Some readers have suggested that Knausgaard unforgivably betrayed his friends and family by exposing their private lives to public scrutiny and the publication of *My Struggle* prompted his uncle to threaten a lawsuit. Even Knausgaard himself admits in interview that he has achieved his success by sacrificing his relationships with friends and family.

My Struggle is interesting to compare to The Neapolitan quartet as the two series share an intensity of tone and seem to blur the distinction between autobiography and fiction. Presuming that much of Ferrante's subject matter is autobiographical, the reception of Knausgaard's work also offers an interesting insight into why Ferrante has chosen to conceal her identity.

BIBLIOGRAPHY

Books

Ferrante, Elena. *My Brilliant Friend*, Europa Editions, 2011 (translation by Ann Goldstein)

Ferrante, Elena. *The Story of a New Name*, Europa Editions, 2013 (translation by Ann Goldstein)

Ferrante, Elena. *Those Who Leave and Those Who Stay*, Europa Editions, 2013 (translation by Ann Goldstein)

Ferrante, Elena. *The Story of the Lost Child* Europa Editions, 2015 (translation by Ann Goldstein)

Articles

Sarah Begley. 'The historical truth behind Elena Ferrante's Neapolitan novels.' *Time Magazine*, 31 August 2015

Joanna Biggs. 'I was blind, she a falcon.' *The London Review of Books*, 10 September 2015

Nora Caplan-Bricker. 'How Jane Austen Helped Inspire Elena Ferrante's Disappearing Act.' *Slate*, 20 October 2015

Irene Caselli. 'The realism of Elena Ferrante's Naples.' CITYLAB, 2 September 2015

Rachel Donadio. 'Italy's Great, Mysterious Storyteller.' *The New York Review of Books*, 18 December 2014

Rachel Donadio. 'Writing has always been a great struggle for me: Q & A with Elena Ferrante.' *The New York Times*, 9 December 2014

Katrina Dodson. 'The Face of Ferrante: Katrina Dodson Interviews Ann Goldstein.' *Guernica Magazine*

Joan Frank. 'The Story of a New Name: review.' The San Francisco Chronicle, 13 December 2013

David Kurnick. 'FERRANTE, IN HISTORY.' *Public Books*, 15 December 2015

Meghan O'Rourke. 'Elena Ferrante: the global literary sensation nobody knows.' *The Guardian*, 31 October 2014

Deborah Orr. 'Elena Ferrante: 'Anonymity lets me concentrate exclusively on writing.' *The Guardian*, 19 February 2016

Minna Proctor. 'A Woman Escaped.' *Bookforum*, February 2014
Susanna Sonnenberg. 'My Brilliant Friend by Elena Ferrante.' *The San Francisco Chronicle*, 1 October 2012

Catherine Taylor. '*Those Who Leave and Those Who Stay* by Elena Ferrante Review: High Stakes Literature.' *The Telegraph*, 9 September 2014

Simon Willis. 'The grandmaster of Naples.' *Intelligent Life Magazine*, December 2013

James Wood. 'Women on the verge: the fiction of Elena Ferrante.' *The New Yorker*, 21 January 2013

Websites

www.elenaferrante.com

www.historylearningsite.co.uk/modern-world-history

90

Further Titles in The Reading Room Series

The Book Thief (Markus Zusak): A Guide for Book Clubs

The Fault in Our Stars (John Green): A Guide for Book Clubs

Frankenstein (Mary Shelley): A Guide for Book Clubs

The Girl on the Train (Paula Hawkins): A Guide for Book Clubs

Go Set a Watchman (Harper Lee): A Guide for Readers

A God in Ruins (Kate Atkinson): A Guide for Book Clubs

The Goldfinch (Donna Tartt): A Guide for Book Clubs

Gone Girl (Gillian Flynn): A Guide for Book Clubs

The Great Gatsby (F. Scott Fitzgerald): A Guide for Book Clubs

The Grownup (Gillian Flynn): A Guide for Book Clubs

The Guernsey Literary and Potato Peel Pie Society (Mary Ann Shaffer & Annie Burrows): A Guide for Book Clubs

The Heart Goes Last (Margaret Atwood): A Guide for Book Clubs

The Husband's Secret (Liane Moriarty): A Guide for Book Clubs

I Know Why the Caged Bird Sings (Maya Angelou): A Guide for Book Clubs

The Light between Oceans (M.L. Stedman): A Guide for Book Clubs

My Name is Lucy Barton (Elizabeth Strout): A Guide for Book Clubs

The Narrow Road to the Deep North (Richard Flanagan): A Guide for Book Clubs

The Paying Guests (Sarah Waters): A Guide for Book Clubs

The Secret History (Donna Tartt): A Guide for Book Clubs

The Storied Life of A.J. Fikry (Gabrielle Zevin): A Guide for Book Clubs

The Sympathizer (Viet Thanh Nguyen): A Guide for Book Clubs

For more details of all of these books and more please visit:

www.amazon.com/author/kathryncope

ABOUT THE AUTHOR

Kathryn Cope graduated in English Literature from Manchester University and obtained her Master's in contemporary fiction from the University of York. She is a reviewer and author of The Reading Room Book Group Guides. She lives in the Peak District with her husband and son.

www.amazon.com/author/kathryncope

65569004R00055

Made in the USA
Middletown, DE
28 February 2018